LIBRARY OF SOUTHERN CIVILIZATION

LEWIS P. SIMPSON, EDITOR

My Passage at the New Orleans *Tribune*

My Passage at the New Orleans *Tribune*

A MEMOIR OF THE CIVIL WAR ERA

Jean-Charles Houzeau

EDITED, WITH AN INTRODUCTION, BY

DAVID C. RANKIN

TRANSLATED BY GERARD F. DENAULT

Louisiana State University Press

Baton Rouge and London

Copyright © 1984 by Louisiana State University Press
ALL RIGHTS RESERVED
Manufactured in the United States of America
Designer: Barbara Werden
Typeface: Linotron Fournier
Typesetter: G & S Typesetters, Inc.

LIBRARY OF CONGRESS CATALOGING IN PUBLICATION DATA

Houzeau, Jean-Charles, 1820–1888.
My passage at the New Orleans Tribune.

(Library of Southern civilization)
Translation of: Mon passage à la Tribune de la
Nouvelle-Orléans
Includes index.
1. Houzeau, Jean-Charles, 1820–1888. 2. Journalists—
Louisiana—New Orleans—Biography. 3. New Orleans
Tribune. 4. Creoles—Louisiana—New Orleans. 5. New
Orleans (La.)—Riot, 1866. I. Rankin, David C.
II. Title. III. Series
PN4874.H68A3613   1984   070.4'1'092'4 [B]   84-7185
ISBN 0-8071-1178-3

Frontispiece: Jean-Charles Houzeau.
Reprinted from *Ciel et terre*, IX (1888–89).

FOR SALLY

Contents

Illustrations

Acknowledgments

MANY PEOPLE and institutions have contributed to the preparation of *My Passage at the New Orleans Tribune* for publication. I would like, first, to thank Daniel Aaron for encouraging me to pursue this project while I was a Visiting Fellow in the Program in the History of American Civilization at Harvard University. It is also a pleasure to acknowledge the unflagging support, sage advice, and meticulous editing provided by Leslie Phillabaum, Beverly Jarrett, and Margaret Fisher Dalrymple of Louisiana State University Press.

I am equally grateful to the archivists who shared with me their knowledge of Houzeau's voluminous papers. These include André Uyttebrouck of the Université Libre de Bruxelles; Jean-Luc De Paepe of the Académie Royale des Sciences, des Lettres et des Beaux-Arts de Belgique, who not only introduced me to some of Houzeau's most revealing letters but also shared his elegant office with my three-year-old son; and especially Lisette Danckaert of the Centre National d'Histoire des Sciences at the Bibliothèque Royale Albert 1er. Ms. Danckaert, Hosam Elkhadem, and the rest of the staff at the Centre assisted me far beyond the call of duty and made my stay in Brussels one that I will always cherish.

For answering a variety of questions about Houzeau and his memoir I would also like to thank David H. De Vorkin of the National Air and Space Museum in Washington, D.C., Gary S. Dunbar of the University of California at Los Angeles, Joseph Ewan of Tulane University, Owen Gingerich of the Center for Astrophysics at Harvard University, Charles E. Murgia of the University of California at Berkeley, and Francis Sartorius of the Institut d'Études Européennes at the Université Libre de Bruxelles. I owe a special debt to Richard I. Frank of the University of California at Irvine for helping track down some of Houzeau's more obscure classical allusions and to Gerard F. Denault of Harvard University for not only translating Houzeau's memoir but also providing im-, portant information on nineteenth-century France. Ronald G. Suny, my former colleague at Oberlin College, explained the nuances of early socialist thought, and Joseph Logsdon of the University of New Orleans, in an act of remarkable generosity, shared with me his notes from Houzeau's papers at the Bibliothèque Royale Albert 1 er. George Slusser of the University of California at Riverside also provided valuable assistance in the preparation of Houzeau's memoir for publication.

I am particularly indebted to David Herbert Donald of Harvard University and Michael P. Johnson of the University of California at Irvine for reading the entire manuscript and offering excellent suggestions for its improvement. But my greatest debt is to my wife Sally, who helped translate Houzeau's prose and improve mine. The dedication is poor payment for her labor, and her patience.

My Passage at the New Orleans *Tribune*

Introduction

ANY AMERICANS know the story of John Howard Griffin, the white journalist who in 1959 artificially darkened his skin and wandered through the streets of New Orleans disguised as a Negro. *Black Like Me*, Griffin's moving account of what it was like to be a Negro in the Deep South on the eve of the Civil Rights Movement, became a nationwide best-seller, and Griffin himself became a celebrity.

Few people, on the other hand, know that a white Belgian named Jean-Charles Houzeau anticipated Griffin's story by nearly a century. Like Griffin, Houzeau came to New Orleans at the beginning of a great civil rights struggle. He also came as a journalist, passed for black, and later published an impassioned account of his experiences. His memoir foreshadows that of Griffin in uncanny ways. Griffin, for instance, wrote in 1960 that "the real story [of the Negro] is the universal one of men who destroy the souls and bodies of other men. . . . It is the story of the persecuted, the defrauded, the feared and detested. I could have been a Jew in Germany, a Mexican in a number of states, or a member of any 'inferior' group. Only the details would have differed. The story would be the same." Houzeau, in a strikingly similar passage, observed in 1870 that the Negro cause "was after all only one chapter in the great universal fight of the oppressed of all colors and nations. Whether the victim is called a serf in Russia, peasant in Austria, Jew in Prussia, proletarian in France, pariah in

India, Negro in the United States, at heart it is the same denial of justice."

But there were differences as well as similarities in the experiences of these two men, differences that make Houzeau's memoir all the more fascinating. To pass for black, Griffin darkened his skin under the direction of a dermatologist, while Houzeau was naturally of dark complexion and, in his words, simply "never sought to deny the rumor that I had African blood in my veins." Physically, then, Houzeau was able to pass for as long as he wanted, and he did so for three and a half years. Griffin, however, could remain black only until his medication wore off; in the end, despite repeated applications of stain, he was able to pass for less than a month. Moreover, Griffin went to New Orleans looking for a story, whereas Houzeau went there to write newspaper stories. Indeed, it is one of the great ironies of the Reconstruction era that the editor of the New Orleans *Tribune*, the first black daily in America, was a white Belgian. Finally, soon after leaving New Orleans Griffin flew off to the nation's major media centers, and his book went on to sell over five million copies. In contrast, when Houzeau left New Orleans in 1868 he sailed to Jamaica, where he settled on an isolated banana farm, and his memoir, one of the most extraordinary documents in the history of the South, was buried in an obscure nineteenth-century Belgian periodical.[1]

JEAN-CHARLES-HIPPOLYTE-JOSEPH HOUZEAU DE LEHAIE was born into an old and aristocratic Belgian family on October 7, 1820, at the Ermitage de Saint-Barthélemy, a magnificent estate

1. John Howard Griffin, *Black Like Me* (1960; New York, 1976), 5 and *passim*; J.-C. Houzeau, "Le journal noir, aux États-Unis, de 1863 à 1870," *Revue de Belgique*, XI (May 15, 1872), 5–28 (quotation on p. 8), and (June 15, 1872), 97–122. Houzeau's two-part article was a reprint of a pamphlet that he had published in 1870 under the title, "Mon passage à la *Tribune* de la Nouvelle-Orléans." Hereinafter I refer to Houzeau's memoir as "My Passage," and all subsequent page num-

on the outskirts of Mons. His father, though listed in the annual register of Belgian nobles, was something of a radical. An agnostic who admired Diderot and the French Encyclopedists, he was a firm believer in the great principles that inspired the French revolutionaries of 1789. His mother, the daughter of a French physician and a patron of the fine arts, embraced revolutionary values even more fervently than his father. Under the tutelage of his parents, Houzeau studied privately at home in the superb library that his father, a member of the Société des Bibliophiles Belges, had built at the Ermitage. During the winter, when the family moved to Paris, he spent long hours at the Bibliothèque Nationale and lived at the Sorbonne with his uncle, who was vice-rector of the University of Paris.[2]

---

bers are from the translated version that follows this Introduction. I have been unable to locate a copy of the original pamphlet.

2. For a discussion of the Houzeau estate, see Ernest Matthieu, "L'Ermitage de Saint-Barthélemy à Mons," *Annales du cercle archéologique de Mons*, XXXVIII (1909), 1–101. In preparing the following sketch of Houzeau, I have drawn upon Joseph Nyns-Lagye, "Jean-Charles Houzeau, sa vie et ses oeuvres," *Revue pédagogique belge*, I (1888), 390–416; Albert B. M. Lancaster, "J.-C. Houzeau: Notes biographiques," in J.-C. Houzeau and A. Lancaster, *Bibliographie générale de l'astronomie* (2 vols.; Brussels, 1880–89), I, pt. 2, i–cxx; J.-B.-J. Liagre, "Notice sur Jean-Charles Houzeau," *Annuaire de l'académie royale des sciences, des lettres et des beaux-arts de Belgique*, LVI (1890), 207–310; Pol Swings, "Jean-Charles Houzeau de Lehaie," in the Belgian *Biographie nationale*, XXIX, supplément 1 (1957), 694–99. Paul Brien's essay on Houzeau in his *Florilège des sciences en Belgique pendant le XIXᵉ siècle et le début du XX* (Brussels, 1967), 69–96, is essentially a reprint of passages from Liagre's 1890 biography. Important information on the Houzeau family may be found in Clovis Piérard's biography of Houzeau's nephew, "Le naturaliste Jean Houzeau de Lahaie et sa famille," *Mémoires et publications de la société des sciences, des arts et des lettres du Hainaut*, LXXIV (1960), 73–129. Other helpful material is available in the testimonies given at the time of Houzeau's death by Charles Ruelens, J.-B.-J. Liagre, Victor Arnould, F. Folie, César De Paepe, Jules Janssen, and others in Société Royale Belge de Géographie, *Bulletin*, XII (1888), 365–73, and *Ciel et terre*, IX (1888–89), 225, 249–70, 318, 368–70.

There is no satisfactory biographical study of Houzeau in English. Brief sketches may be found in *Popular Science Monthly*, XXXVIII (1891), 544–52, where Lancaster's 1889 biography is translated and summarized; Edward L. Tinker, "Bibliography of the French Newspapers and Periodicals of Louisiana," *Pro-

Houzeau proved to be an able but independent student. After winning a silver medal for his outstanding work at the Collège de Mons, he enrolled in 1837 in the Faculty of Sciences at the Free University of Brussels. Shortly thereafter, however, he failed his university examinations and returned home. Although he later attended the University of Paris from 1840 through 1841, Houzeau never earned a formal degree. A close friend explained: "An inquiring, original, and independent spirit, he was very interested in scientific, political and social studies, but he could never submit himself to university discipline."[3]

---

ceedings of the American Antiquarian Society, New Series, XLII (1933), 265–66, 320; Edward L. Tinker, Creole City: Its Past and Its People (New York, 1953), 107–21, a popular history without references; Finnian P. Leavens, "L'Union and the New Orleans Tribune and Louisiana Reconstruction" (M.A. thesis, Louisiana State University, 1966), ch. 3; Geraldine M. McTigue, "Forms of Racial Interaction in Louisiana, 1860–1880" (Ph.D. dissertation, Yale University, 1975), 41–51; William P. Connor, "Reconstruction Rebels: The New Orleans Tribune in Post-War Louisiana," Louisiana History, XXI (1980), 162–79, a study that suffers from a number of factual errors. The basis of Tinker's pioneering but uncritical and sometimes inaccurate sketches of Houzeau may be reconstructed by consulting his notebook labeled "New Orleans Newspapers" and his unlabeled notebook containing biographical information on various newspapermen in the Edward Laroque Tinker Collection, Humanities Research Center, University of Texas, Austin, Texas. Neither is there a modern study that draws upon Houzeau's voluminous correspondence in Belgium. Maurice Chazin, who knew of the papers, promised such a volume in the 1930s, but it has never appeared; see Frank Monaghan, French Travellers in the United States, 1765–1932 (1933; New York, 1961), 50. The major manuscript collections that I have drawn upon in preparing this essay are the J.-B.-J. Liagre Papers, Archives, Académie Royale des Sciences, des Lettres et des Beaux-Arts de Belgique, Brussels, Belgium (cited hereinafter as the Liagre Papers); Correspondance J.-C. Houzeau-N. C. Schmit, Archives, Université Libre de Bruxelles, Brussels, Belgium (cited hereinafter as Correspondance Houzeau-Schmit); and the Jean-Charles Houzeau Papers, Centre National d'Histoire des Sciences, Bibliothèque Royale Albert 1ᵉʳ, Brussels, Belgium (cited hereinafter as Houzeau Papers). The Centre National d'Histoire des Sciences, which is currently preparing Houzeau's papers for publication, has photocopies of Houzeau's letters to his parents and brother; the originals are still held by the Houzeau family and housed at l'Ermitage de Saint-Barthélemy. There are in these three manuscript collections roughly 1,500 Houzeau letters dating from 1838 to 1888.

3. Liagre, "Notice," 210.

Upon his departure from the Free University of Brussels, Houzeau began a career as a journalist. In 1839, at the age of nineteen, he published a hundred-page pamphlet entitled *Des turbines, de leur construction, du calcul de leur puissance et de leur application à l'industrie.* This essay demonstrated his lifelong ability to popularize technical knowledge and set forth his belief that scientific progress would result in social progress.[4] Houzeau was nevertheless troubled by the distressing social consequences that often accompanied the application of scientific knowledge to daily life. In Belgium, the first European ˙nation to industrialize, he had plenty of evidence that the consequences could be grim indeed. Thus, in a series of articles dealing with industrialization in the Brussels *L'Émancipation* between 1838 and 1841, Houzeau often focused upon topics such as the explosion of steam engines, the dangers of coal mining, child labor in factories, and the health and education of unskilled laborers.

In the early 1840s Houzeau also began publishing scholarly essays on astronomy. His interest in the heavens dated from childhood when, before he could read or write, he made from bits of candy geometrical forms representing various constellations. At eighteen he built with his own hands a small observatory, complete with a wall quadrant and a telescope distinguished by lenses ground in Paris. His first significant publication in astronomy appeared in 1843 in the German journal *Astronomische Nachrichten.* It was a note on zodiacal light which Houzeau's idol, Alexander von Humboldt, soon cited in his monumental study of the *Cosmos.*[5] The following year Houzeau published an article of major impor-

4. For background to Houzeau's belief that scientific knowledge could solve social problems, see Nell Eurich, *Science in Utopia: A Mighty Design* (Cambridge, Mass., 1967).

5. "Schreiben des Herrn J. C. Houzeau an den Herausgeber," *Astronomische Nachrichten*, XXI (1843), 183–90; Alexander von Humboldt, *Cosmos: A Sketch of a Physical Description of the Universe*, trans. E. C. Otté (2 vols.; New York, 1850), I,

tance on double stars. It drew both praise and detailed criticism from Sir John Herschel, C. P. Smyth, Yvon Villarceau, and other leading astronomers. Two years later, as his reputation as a brilliant young astronomer spread, Houzeau was appointed an assistant astronomer at the Royal Observatory in Brussels.

Not long after joining the observatory, Houzeau diverted his attention from astronomy to politics until finally, like so many intellectuals, he became absorbed in the great political and philosophical debates that swept across Europe in 1848. He began by writing articles in the liberal press advocating public education, workmen's compensation, and the right to assemble. He then joined and became an officer in the Phalange, a secret Belgian society dedicated to democratic ideals. Outraged and further radicalized by the conservative Louis-Napoleon Bonaparte's landslide election in France in December, 1848, he published a series of unsigned polemics in the liberal newspaper *Le Débat Social* and advised the members of the Phalange: "Our place . . . today is to join the ranks of the proletariat. It will do us no more good to write and to speak for the bourgeoisie. . . . For my part, I renounce all work, all society, where one does not frankly embrace the flag of the proletariat." Houzeau placed his hope for the future in the diffusion of scientific knowledge and socialism. "Forward! Spread the word!" he exhorted his coworkers. "It is at the door of the people that scientific knowledge and its application must be placed. When a generation has grown up on socialist teachings and workers' associations, there will be a revolution in its ideas and we will have only to harvest the ripened fruit." Eventually, he predicted, all obstacles would be overcome, "for one does not stop the flow of rivers." But three months after writing these optimistic lines, Houzeau presided over a democratic rally that was attacked

---

14n. For a discussion of von Humboldt's profound influence upon Houzeau, see Lancaster, "J.-C. Houzeau," xvii–xix.

and routed by a vicious mob of royalists. He survived the attack, as he would the New Orleans Riot of 1866, by escaping through a back door, and subsequently defended the gathering as being fully in accordance with the Belgian constitution. Government officials, who had been monitoring his activities, thought otherwise. At their insistence, Houzeau was dismissed from his post at the Royal Observatory on April 6, 1849.[6]

Houzeau's dismissal afforded him the opportunity to travel and write. In the next few years he spent time in Germany, Austria, Czechoslovakia, Switzerland, England, and especially France, where he lived for most of the 1850s and secretly married a working-class girl in 1851.[7] During his stay in Paris, Houzeau put

6. Houzeau to G. Mathieu, December 14, 1848, quoted in Hubert Wouters (ed.), *Documenten betreffende de geschiedenis der arbeidersbeweging (1831–53)* (3 vols; Louvain, 1963), II, 715–18. For evidence and a discussion of Houzeau's active participation in the upheavals of 1848–1849, see *ibid.*, II, 657, 701–702, 736, 752, 766–67, 770, 777, 782–83, 785–86, 788, 806, 808, 816, 829; Louis Bertrand, *Histoire de la démocratie & du socialisme en Belgique depuis 1830* (2 vols.; Brussels, 1906–1907), I, 390–404. For a discussion of the influence of Karl Marx, Mikhail Bakunin, Alexander Herzen, Louis Blanc, and especially P.-J. Proudhon upon the young Belgian radicals of 1848–1849, see Bertrand, *Histoire de la démocratie*, II, ch. 3. Houzeau would continue in later years to speak of Proudhon and his work, and Proudhon would refer to Houzeau as a "superior mind." Houzeau to his parents, June 3, 8, 1859, Houzeau to his father, August 24, 1872, all in Houzeau Papers.

Houzeau remained bitter about his dismissal for many years. "I do not think," he wrote to Victor Bouvy from New Orleans on November 18, 1864, "that our government has for a member of its [Royal] Academy the generosity that the Negroes of America have for a sympathetic immigrant who came to them from they do not know where." In Liagre Papers.

7. Houzeau's marriage, according to a close friend, "was an amicable association, in which the woman's principal mission was to spare the man the small details of material existence." He did not take his wife with him to America in 1857, and he did not return for her funeral in December, 1865. He did, however, send her money regularly and said that except for his commitment to the Negroes of New Orleans he would have returned during her long and painful battle against cancer. Later, after returning to Belgium in 1876, Houzeau married his first wife's sister-in-law. The Belgian pedagogue Alexis Sluys claimed in 1925 that Houzeau had a Negro wife living with him after his return to Belgium, but his assertion is improbable, and I have found no evidence to corroborate it. Whether Houzeau had a

in endless hours at the Bibliothèque Nationale and grew increasingly confident that he was destined to produce works of major importance. In February, 1852, he confided in his parents: "Truly, I can say this in an intimate letter, I sense more and more my superiority."[8] The articles that he was publishing at the time were in fact of superior quality and included studies of the colonization of Pitcairn Island in the South Pacific, the history of astronomy in the United States, the aberrations of the human mind, and the triangulation of Belgium. His books ranged from the popular *Physique du globe et météorologie* (1851) and *Règles de climatologie* (1853), which was translated into German in 1861, to the scholarly *Essai d'une géographie physique de la Belgique, au point de vue de l'histoire et de la description du globe* (1854) and *Histoire du sol de l'Europe* (1857). These last two volumes, according to the president of the Belgian Royal Academy of Sciences, Letters, and Fine Arts, were "equal in knowledge as well as style to those from the pen of von Humboldt."[9] In 1856, at age thirty-six, Houzeau was elected a member of the Belgian Royal Academy.

A year after his election to the academy, Houzeau decided to visit America. In July, 1857, he moved to London, where he studied at the British Museum and worked as a typographer; two months later he boarded a small ship manned by five white of-

---

Negro wife (or mistress) in New Orleans or Jamaica is unknown, but if so, he never mentions her in his correspondence. Houzeau did, on the other hand, speak openly of his two adopted Negro sons, neither of whom could possibly have been his natural child. Liagre, "Notice," 236–37; Houzeau to Victor Bouvy, November 18, 1864, February 18, March 1, December 7, 1865, January 24, 1866, all in Liagre Papers; Alexis Sluys to Fernand Héger, August 4, 1925, in Armoire blindée no. 5, Archives, Université Libre de Bruxelles, Brussels, Belgium.

8. Houzeau to his parents, February 20, 1852, in Houzeau Papers.

9. J.-B.-J. Liagre in Société Royale Belge de Géographie, *Bulletin*, XII (1888), 368. See also the long and laudatory review of *Histoire du sol de l'Europe* by the eminent French geographer Elisée Reclus entitled "Considérations sur quelques faits de géologie et d'ethnologie," *Revue philosophique et religieuse*, IX (1858), 218–27.

ficers and fifteen Negro sailors and jammed with immigrants bound for the New World. He reached New Orleans on October 28. Like many other nineteenth-century naturalists, Houzeau was headed for the prairies of Texas, but after his arrival he decided to stay in New Orleans long enough to complete what he termed "my apprenticeship for American life." This included studying English classics at night and American laws in the daytime. He also paid close attention to the city of New Orleans, which he instructed his father to pronounce "niou-orlinns." Although visitors usually took New Orleans for a French city, Houzeau found that "the sole vestige of French ideas is that shops are open on Sunday." He was impressed, however, by the city's Negro population, which included roughly 10,000 free coloreds and 15,000 slaves. The Negroes were "very decent, very kind, very polite, and generally superior to the whites in ordinary relations." Initially, he found the condition of the slaves indistinguishable from that of the free coloreds, improving every day, and better than that of workers and servants in Europe. He appears also to have believed the white Louisianians who assured him that slavery was dissolving into "*temporary servitude*"; indeed, he informed his parents in January, 1858, that "the difficulty is not *abolition*; the South favors it more than one might think." Houzeau was hopeful that abolition would come quickly and voluntarily, for slavery was a "shameful evil," "introduced by the Spanish and the French," that was inconsistent with American democracy. It was an anomaly in a nation that, five months after his arrival, he confessed to "loving . . . for the moral and material well-being that it is able to pour forth upon all its children."[10]

10. Houzeau to his parents, October 30, November 7, 28, 1857, January 23, February 14, 1858, Houzeau to his father, October 18, 1864, all in Houzeau Papers; Houzeau, "Correspondance d'Amérique," *Revue trimestrielle*, XVIII (April 1858), 293–307. Houzeau wrote home that "the great merit of the American government is having nothing that resembles either classes or castes. There are

Houzeau's optimism faded after emigrating to Texas in the spring of 1858. The next four years, when he traveled throughout the southern and western portions of the state working as a land surveyor, gathering botanical and geological specimens, making astronomical observations, and taking copious notes on the behavior of frontier men and animals, were exhilarating, to be sure. In fact, he told friends that he could have continued in this "vagabond existence" for the rest of his life. But as sectional tensions mounted in the late 1850s, Houzeau grew increasingly pessimistic about the possibility of Americans amicably solving the problem of slavery.[11]

When civil war finally did erupt in April, 1861, Houzeau declared that he would cut off his right hand rather than aid the Confederate cause. "In the midst of a world devoted to profit, where the passions of avarice know neither limits nor decency," he wrote, "I refuse to allow myself to be corrupted. . . . We must not repudiate the most sublime and most saintly attributes of our nature: the aptitude for progress, the conscience of right, the idea

---

no corporations whose interests are distinct from those of the masses. There is no clergy, no army, no body of magistrates, no permanent public functionaries, no aristocracy of birth or wealth. What makes the *parvenu* insufferable in Europe is that he is assured the permanence of his rank, whereas the American speculator knows that he can fall in a day. . . . What people! What noble sentiments of tolerance, of grandeur, of union, of enthusiasm! Is there anything this nation will not be capable of doing one day?" Houzeau to his parents, February 14, 1858, n.d. [March, 1858?], both in Houzeau Papers. During his stay in the Americas, Houzeau sent twenty-five articles describing the United States, Mexico, and Jamaica to the Belgian periodical *Revue trimestrielle*. His topics included: religious revivals and Mormonism (XX [October, 1858], 263–84); southern agriculture and slavery (XXII [April, 1859], 307–12); the election of 1860 and secession (XXX [April, 1861], 308–27); life in Mexico (XXXVI [October, 1862], 432–47); the assassination of Lincoln (2nd ser., VII [July, 1865], 333–39); and colonialism in Jamaica (2nd ser., XX [January, 1869], 188–99). On the naturalist invasion of Texas, see Samuel W. Geiser, *Naturalists of the Frontier* (Dallas, 1948). Geiser provides bibliography on Houzeau in his "Men of Science in Texas, 1820–1880: II," *Field and Laboratory*, XXVII (1959), 45.
    11. Lancaster, "J.-C. Houzeau," xxxvii.

of morality." Instead of fighting for slavery, Houzeau joined an underground movement that helped fugitive slaves and persecuted Unionists escape from Texas. About to be arrested for assisting in the escape of Charles Anderson, brother of the Union major who had surrendered at Fort Sumter, Houzeau decided in February, 1862, to make a run for Mexico. Donning sombrero and serape, sporting a deep tan acquired on the prairie, speaking tolerable Spanish, and going by the name Carlos Uzo, he passed himself off as a Mexican wagoner and made his way south across the border to Matamoros. He remained stranded in Mexico from March 20, 1862, until January 12, 1863, when, because of his membership in the Belgian Royal Academy, he was allowed to sail for New Orleans, which was now under Federal control, on the Union warship *Kensington*.[12]

Houzeau remained in New Orleans for five months before heading for Philadelphia, where he spent most of his time studying Herodotus, Huxley, Hume, Cellini, Darwin, and anyone else whose work might contribute in some way to the completion of a book he was writing on the mental faculties of men and animals. But Houzeau did not finish his manuscript in Philadelphia, for in November, 1864, he was on his way back to New Orleans to become editor of the *Tribune*. This, his third visit to the Crescent City in seven years, lasted until May, 1868, when he sailed for Jamaica, settled on a small farm, and in 1872 finally published his *Études sur les facultés mentales des animaux comparées à celles de l'homme.*[13]

12. Houzeau to his parents, April 16, 1862, February 1, 1863, both in Houzeau Papers; Houzeau to N. C. Schmit, February 1, 1863, in Correspondance Houzeau-Schmit; Houzeau, "Correspondance d'Amérique," *Revue trimestrielle*, XXXV (July, 1862), 170–238. Upon arriving in Matamoros, Houzeau was taken in by a free colored émigré from Louisiana. He and his white wife, Houzeau later wrote, "welcomed me with a warmth that I will never forget." "Correspondance d'Amérique" (July, 1862), 233.

13. Houzeau to his mother, November 11, 1863, Houzeau to his brother Au-

In this massive two-volume study, based largely upon data gathered in Texas and Mexico, Houzeau wrote confidently of the day when "the entire population of the world, like a single family, diversified but united," would speak the same language. He declared his belief that "humanity progresses without interruption" and that environment, not heredity, determined intellectual and moral development. Physical type, Houzeau argued, could be handed down from parent to child. "But if one wants to speak of dynasties of intelligence, succession is not from father to son; it passes from master to disciple. It is not by genealogies but by schools that knowledge is transmitted." His experiences as a teacher of black, brown, and white children in Jamaica confirmed this "law of nature." In appraising the capacity of his students to learn, he could "see nothing—at least nothing clearly and unmistakably discernible—that can be referred to the differences of race. . . . The rate of improvement is due almost entirely to the relative elevation of the parental circle in which children live—the home influence." Aware that his findings ran against the prevailing tide of scholarly opinion, Houzeau predicted that his conclusions would "probably appear strange after all that has been said of 'inferior races.'" He held his ground, however, contending that "most of the savan[t]s of Europe have but a very incomplete idea of the mental, and still more of the moral, status of 'inferior societies.'"[14]

guste, June 26, 1864, Houzeau to his parents, August 25, 1864, Houzeau to his father, October 18, 1864, all in Houzeau Papers; Houzeau, *Études sur les facultés mentales des animaux comparées à celles de l'homme* (2 vols.; Mons, 1872). Houzeau wrote to his mother on November 22, 1864, that *Études* was finished except for the "final touches," which he expected to add during his free time in New Orleans. In Houzeau Papers.

14. Houzeau, *Études sur les facultés mentales*, II, 429, 634, 639; Houzeau to W. Lauder Lindsay, n.d., quoted in *Nature*, X (1874), 272. Houzeau published volume one of *Études* anonymously, and his name appeared in parentheses on the title page of volume two. For a discussion of racist thought in nineteenth-century Eu-

One of the most respected European savants to review Houzeau's *Études* was Alfred R. Wallace, co-author with Charles Darwin of the famous paper delivered in 1858 at the Linnaean Society in which the modern theory of evolution was first presented to the world. Wallace, who after exploring Malaysia in the 1860s had predicted the gradual extinction of colored peoples, chided Houzeau for "very imperfectly" treating the subject of "Hereditary Transmission," about which Francis Galton, father of the eugenics movement, had written so persuasively. Although Wallace declared that Houzeau's work "could not for a moment" be compared to that of Darwin or Herbert Spencer, he did conclude that *Études* had "special merits of its own," including "a mass of curious facts, acute observations, and sound reasoning, which fully entitle its author to take high rank among philosophical naturalists." Houzeau doubtless took some pleasure from the review, for in it an eminent biologist had simultaneously acknowledged the importance of his work and dissociated it from the racist writings of Galton and Spencer. The observations of W. Lauder Lindsay, a distinguished Scottish physician, gave Houzeau cause for even greater satisfaction. Lindsay deemed *Études* "on a par with the works of Mr. Darwin" and "one of the most important contributions yet made to the science of comparative psychology." He found *Études* all the more impressive because its author was an

---

rope, see Jacques Barzun, *Race: A Study in Superstition* (New York, 1965), chs. 2–7; George W. Stocking, Jr., *Race, Culture, and Evolution: Essays in the History of Anthropology* (New York, 1968), chs. 2–3; Léon Poliakov, *The Aryan Myth: A History of Racist and Nationalist Ideas in Europe*, trans. Edmund Howard (New York, 1974), chs. 10–11. In the formation of his liberal racial views, Houzeau was influenced by his idol von Humboldt, who wrote in the most famous passage of his multivolume *Cosmos*: "Whilst we maintain the unity of the human species, we at the same time repel the depressing assumption of superior and inferior races of men. There are nations more susceptible of cultivation than others—but none in themselves nobler than others. All are in like degree designed for freedom." Quoted in Stephen Jay Gould, *The Mismeasure of Man* (New York, 1981), 38. See Houzeau, "Correspondance d'Amérique," *Revue trimestrielle*, XXIX (January, 1861), 293.

astronomer who lived on a banana farm in Jamaica. Darwin was also impressed. He cited *Études* several times in *The Descent of Man* and in 1872 sent Houzeau a copy of his latest book, *The Expression of the Emotions in Man and Animals*.[15]

Houzeau stayed on his two-acre farm in a poor and racially mixed region of Jamaica for four years after the publication of *Études*. During that time he and two young Negro boys, who eventually inherited the farm, worked at raising bananas and coffee. Houzeau spent the rest of his time climbing mountains, teaching neighborhood children, and writing books. In 1873 he published his widely read *Le ciel mis à la portée de tout le monde*, which was reprinted in 1877 and again in 1882. In the mid-1870s he published two long articles on calculus and printed on his own press the first 380 pages of *Compagnon du calculateur numérique*. He also undertook the charting of nearly six thousand stars, a project that took him to Panama in late 1875. Upon returning from this trip, Houzeau learned that the staff of the Royal Observatory in Brussels wanted him to replace the recently deceased director of the observatory. But it was by no means certain at first that Houzeau would return to Europe. In the 1860s he had declined a professorship in geology at the Free University of Brussels, and by 1876 he had fallen in love with Jamaica. Neither was it clear that the Belgian government would allow the Royal Observatory to fall under the control of a political and intellectual maverick like Houzeau. Finally, however, King Léopold II agreed to the appointment, and on June 17, 1876, Houzeau became director of the

15. Wallace, "Houzeau on the Faculties of Man and Animals," *Nature*, VI (1872), 469–71; Poliakov, *Aryan Myth*, 291; W. Lauder Lindsay, "Mind in the Lower Animals," *Nature*, VIII (1873), 91–92; Charles Darwin, *The Origin of Species . . . and The Descent of Man and Selection in Relation to Sex* (New York: Modern Library, n.d.), 453, 457, 461, 463, 475, 487; Houzeau to Charles Darwin, February 24, 1873, in Charles Darwin Archives, Cambridge University Library, Cambridge, England.

observatory that had fired him for political reasons twenty-seven years before.[16]

The years of his directorship were busy and productive ones for Houzeau. In 1876 he published *L'étude de la nature, ses charmes et ses dangers*, a volume that the secretary of the Belgian Royal Academy described as a unique blend of science, philosophy, and poetry. The following year he began simultaneously to modernize the observatory by upgrading its staff and equipment and to democratize the observatory by opening its lectures and library to the public. In 1878 he received the prestigious Five-Year Award of the Physical and Mathematical Science Section of the Belgian Royal Academy and served as president of both the Royal Academy and the Belgian Geographical Society. Two years later he represented Belgium at the International Congress of Meteorologists in Rome. In 1882 he led the Belgian expedition to Texas to observe the transit of Venus and published *Vade-mecum de l'astronome*, a 1,144-page bibliography that demonstrated his astonishing erudition and remains to this day an indispensible guide to the history of astronomy.[17]

Houzeau resigned as director of the Royal Observatory in 1883. Although he had revitalized the existing observatory and

16. The two boys were named William Lang and George Hall. William, whom Houzeau described as "very intelligent" and "very attached to me," had worked for Houzeau since the summer of 1867 and sailed with him from New Orleans to Jamaica in May, 1868. Houzeau to his parents, July 4, October 3, 1867, May 9, 1868, all in Houzeau Papers; Houzeau, "De New Orleans à la Jamaïque," *Revue trimestrielle*, 2nd ser., XIX (July, 1868), 223.

Though he at times seemed totally mesmerized by Jamaica's natural beauty, Houzeau was nevertheless keenly aware of the island's grave social and economic problems. They were, he argued in "La Jamaïque et le système colonial," *ibid.*, XX (January, 1869), 188–89, the consequence of a pernicious European colonialism.

17. J.-B.-J. Liagre, *Rapport du jury du concours quinquennal des sciences physiques et mathématiques*, quoted in Lancaster, "J.-C. Houzeau," xcii–xciii. For contemporary comments on the importance of the *Vade-mecum de l'astronome* (Brussels, 1882), see Liagre, "Notice," 282; *Observatory*, XI (1888), 320; *Nature*, XLI (1889), 20.

successfully campaigned for the construction of a new one, Houzeau had grown weary of his life as an administrator and fund raiser. It is, in fact, difficult to imagine a person less suited to becoming a bureaucrat. Houzeau did not drink, smoke, or make small talk. He hated to have his picture taken. He found wearing a coat and hat sheer agony, and he detested anything that was formal or pompous. Solemn, independent, and aloof, he never, according to a friend, "showed himself to be affectionate, happy, or lively except in the most intimate relationships."[18]

Houzeau spent his final years working with Albert Lancaster, a young astronomer at the Royal Observatory, on what would become his most important scholarly work, the *Bibliographie générale de l'astronomie*. By the time a second volume appeared in 1889, the *Bibliographie générale* had already established itself as a classic. The president of the Belgian Royal Academy singled out Houzeau's style in the 310-page introduction for special praise, describing it as a masterful combination "of exactitude and elegance, of gravity and poetry." But the enduring contribution of the work was a massive bibliography—volume one alone contained nearly 16,000 citations—that attempted no less than a complete rendering of all published and unpublished manuscripts in the field of astronomy from the Middle Ages through 1880. In 1964 when the *Bibliographie générale* was reprinted in London, Arthur Beer of the

18. Lancaster, "J.-C. Houzeau," cv. It became evident soon after Houzeau's return to the Royal Observatory that he did not enjoy the life of a bureaucrat. Indeed, in June, 1878, barely two years after assuming the directorship, he took a five-month leave of absence and sailed back to Jamaica. His friends thought he would never return. Later, at his funeral, J.-B.-J. Liagre observed: "But Houzeau was not the man for official position and publicity; the fine details of administration, the requirements of etiquette which he had to meet as head of an important establishment, the campaigns, even the solicitations which he had sometimes to make to gain his ends—these were repugnant to the direct but inflexible nature of the director of our Observatory." *Ibid.*, xcvi; Liagre is quoted in Société Royale Belge de Géographie, *Bulletin*, XII (1888), 372.

Cambridge University Observatories pronounced it "the fundamental bibliographical basis of astronomy." He also despaired that there "perhaps never" would be another Houzeau.[19]

Houzeau died on July 12, 1888, of a tropical disease that he had apparently contracted in Panama. The funeral, which was presided over by his brother Auguste,[20] a member of the Belgian Chamber of Representatives, was held in a bare room in Houzeau's modest home on the outskirts of Brussels. Eulogists included not only dignitaries such as the director of the Royal Observatory, the president of the Royal Academy, and the president of the Belgian Geographical Society, but also Victor Arnould of the Society of Free Thinkers and César De Paepe of the Labor Party. Arnould, who was an editor of the socialist newspaper *La Liberté*, praised Houzeau as "the complete man, embracing the entire cycle of thought and action," whose hopes were "in the future of the little people, of the suffering, of the humble and unknown workers." De Paepe, the great Belgian socialist, recalled that "his natural goodness, the innate sentiments of altruism and especially of sympathy for all who suffer, had, from an early date, made Houzeau the defender of all the oppressed, the friend of all the disinherited of society. He was a socialist by temperament and by instinct; but the study of the positive sciences . . . made him a scientific social-

19. Houzeau and Lancaster, *Bibliographie générale*, vols. I–II; J.-B.-J. Liagre review of *Bibliographie générale* in *Ciel et terre*, VIII (1887–88), 329; Beer is quoted in J.-C. Houzeau and A. Lancaster, *General Bibliography of Astronomy to the Year 1880*, ed. D. W. Dewhirst (2 vols.; London, 1964), I, viii. For an evaluation of Houzeau's bibliographical works and his lofty place in the history of Belgian astronomy, see Raymond Coutrez, "Esquisse d'une histoire de l'astronomie et science connexes en Belgique pendant le XIXᵉ siècle et le début de XXᵉ," in Brien, *Florilège des sciences*, 23–42.

20. Houzeau's brother Charles-Auguste-Benjamin-Hippolyte (1832–1922) was a political liberal and ardent advocate of public education and universal suffrage in the Chamber of Representatives, where he served from 1882 through 1894. He was also for many years a professor at the École des Mines in Mons. Piérard, "Le naturaliste Jean Houzeau," 77, 91–99.

ist, whose convictions rested on unshakeable foundations." De Paepe concluded his eulogy to this "ardent apostle of 1848" by predicting that "Belgian workers will forever venerate the memory of this illustrious savant, this honest and good man." After the service Houzeau was buried, as he had instructed, in a pauper's grave without a headstone.[21]

Tributes from other cities where Houzeau had lived soon appeared. In Mons, an avenue was named after him and a monument was built in his honor. In Paris, the president of the Academy of Science praised Houzeau as a "great scientist" who was "devoted to absolute justice and truth," and the founder of the French Astronomical Society described him as "an independent man" who had "devoted his entire life to the cause of PROGRESS." But in New Orleans, where Houzeau had repeatedly risked his life in the struggle for justice, truth, and progress, there was no mention of his death.[22]

"NEW ORLEANS is greatly transformed," Houzeau wrote to his parents after arriving there from Mexico in early 1863. Captured by Union forces in April, 1862, southern Louisiana was now a region, according to Houzeau, where planters were impoverished, plantations confiscated, "seigneurial rights" abolished, slaves freed, Negroes armed, and "social distinctions based upon color"

21. Excerpts from Arnould's eulogy may be found in *Ciel et terre*, IX (1888–89), 263–64; excerpts from De Paepe may be found in *ibid.*, 264–65, and in Bertrand, *Histoire*, I, 404. Houzeau's collaborator Albert Lancaster echoed the sentiments expressed by Arnould and De Paepe when he wrote in 1889 that Houzeau "was throughout his life given to generous ideas, dreaming of the equality of man and the disappearance of all the distinctions of caste, of wealth, etc. . . . From his youth, he sought out the company of workers. He wanted to know their sufferings, so he could remedy them." Lancaster, "J.-C. Houzeau," cvii.
22. Jules Janssen's speech before the Paris Academy of Science on August 13, 1888, is reprinted in *Ciel et terre*, IX (1888–89), 368–70; Camille Flammarion's eulogy is reprinted in *Astronomie*, VII (1888), 316–17. I have found no mention of Houzeau's death in the New Orleans press.

destined to vanish. Here, he cried, was "a great revolution, one of the greatest in history." Houzeau tempered his enthusiasm, however, by noting that the planter class was determined in its opposition to any change in traditional relationships, particularly those between blacks and whites. "The prejudice of skin," he warned, "is stronger than the seigneurial rights themselves." He also worried about how the conquering "American Anglo-Saxon element" would use "the irresistible power" at its command. He was, for example, distressed to learn that federal officials were enrolling Negroes in the Union army because of military necessity rather than egalitarian principle. In the end, he cautioned, "Black[s] must save themselves, if they may be saved at all."[23]

At the time Houzeau wrote these words, the New Orleans free colored population had already begun to campaign for equal rights. In September, 1862, a small group of them had founded *L'Union*, a French-language newspaper that was edited by Paul Trévigne, published twice a week, and managed by a board of directors that was elected by shareholders every six months.[24]

---

23. Houzeau to his parents, June 18, 1863, in Houzeau Papers; Houzeau to N. C. Schmit, June 24, July 4, 1863, both in Correspondance Houzeau-Schmit. Houzeau continued to worry about the "prejudice of skin." In early 1865 he wrote that "the planters, thanks to God, are ruined; in time they will be destroyed (I mean that they will be seized as debtors); and their property will pass into other hands and will be divided. It is the revolution in landed property that we saw in 1789. But the nobility of skin retains all its ridiculous pride." Houzeau to "My Dear Friends" [his parents], February 12, 1865, in Houzeau Papers.

24. *L'Union*, June 4, 1863. (*L'Union* and all other newspapers cited hereinafter are from New Orleans unless otherwise noted.) Various errors have crept into the literature concerning the publication of *L'Union*. It was not initially a daily as Mary F. Berry, "Negro Troops in Blue and Gray: The Louisiana Native Guards, 1861–1863," *Louisiana History*, VIII (1967), 176, has stated; nor a weekly as Houzeau, "My Passage," 71, Donald E. Everett, "Demands of the New Orleans Free Colored Population for Political Equality, 1862–1865," *Louisiana Historical Quarterly*, XXXVIII (1955), 49, and Peyton McCrary, *Abraham Lincoln and Reconstruction: The Louisiana Experiment* (Princeton, 1978), 181, have stated; nor a tri-weekly as James M. McPherson, *The Negro's Civil War: How American Negroes Felt and Acted During the War for the Union* (New York, 1965), 346, has stated. *L'Union*

L'Union boldly proclaimed the Declaration of Independence "as the basis of our platform." "Let all friends of Progress unite!" the paper trumpeted in its inaugural editorial. "The hour has come for the struggle of the great humanitarian principles against a vile and sordid interest which gives birth to pride, ambition, hypocrisy, and lying, and silences the conscience, that voice of the heavens which cries endlessly to man: 'You were born for liberty and happiness! Do not deceive yourself in this and do not deceive your brother!'"[25]

Here, then, was precisely the kind of struggle that had always attracted Houzeau. "I understood the situation of colored men in New Orleans," he later wrote. "I easily identified myself with them, for even though the individuals were different, the cause was nothing new or strange to me: on the one hand I found an unjust and privileged ruling class, and on the other an oppressed class that had been trampled underfoot and had no role in society." Three weeks after arriving in New Orleans, Houzeau was writing for *L'Union*. "For the moment," he wrote a Belgian friend on February 21, 1863, "I have become one of the regular (but unpaid) editors of the French newspaper *L'Union*." In May he told his parents that he was still placing his "surplus prose in a French newspaper called *L'Union*." He then began to help man-

---

was initially a biweekly; it became a triweekly on December 23, 1862. McPherson, *Negro's Civil War*, 276, also errs in stating that *L'Union* was bilingual from the outset; and Connor, "Reconstruction Rebels," 162, 163, errs in stating that it was never published in English. The paper was originally published in French; beginning in early July, 1863, it was published in both English and French. Virtually everyone has provided the wrong date for *L'Union*'s final issue, which appeared on July 19, 1864; see, for example, Leavens, "*L'Union*," 52; Charles Vincent, *Black Legislators in Louisiana During Reconstruction* (Baton Rouge, 1976), 24; David C. Rankin, "The Politics of Caste: Free Colored Leadership in New Orleans During the Civil War," in Robert R. Macdonald, John R. Kemp, and Edward F. Haas (eds.), *Louisiana's Black Heritage* (New Orleans, 1979), 131.

25. *L'Union*, September 27, 1862. The translation is from McPherson, *Negro's Civil War*, 276.

age the paper and by July claimed to have "a great part in the administration of the newspaper *L'Union*, organ of the free colored population."[26]

Houzeau's talents were, in fact, quickly recognized by the proprietors of *L'Union*. In early July, for instance, when they sought to persuade the city's free coloreds to volunteer in the defense of New Orleans against possible Confederate attack, the proprietors chose Houzeau to write the appeal. His letter to a Belgian friend leaves no doubt that Houzeau realized the irony of his position. "I cut for you from *L'Union* of the 2d inst.," he wrote on July 4, 1863, "this appeal of the 'colored editors,' written by one of your friends."[27] The threatened attack on New Orleans never materialized, but according to Houzeau it made white Unionists keenly aware of the importance of the free colored population. To capitalize on this "new influence," he wrote, "*L'Union*'s managers adopted a measure I advocated long since: to have the paper published in both languages, English as well as French." This change, Houzeau predicted, will give the paper's managers "a controlling

26. Houzeau, "My Passage," 75–76; Houzeau to N. C. Schmit, February 21, 1863 (copy), Houzeau to his parents, May 3, June 18, July 24, 1863, all in Houzeau Papers. In a letter to his mother on November 11, 1863, Houzeau reported that if he had remained in New Orleans in the summer of 1863, he would have earned six thousand francs a year "for the direction of the [colored] press." In *ibid.*

27. The appeal was important because the free coloreds had initially hesitated in responding positively to Union General George F. Shepley's request that they help defend the city against possible attack by Confederate forces under the command of General Richard Taylor. "The colored, who had been promised in 1815, in a similar case, the abolition of the Black Code and been deceived," Houzeau explained, "were for a few hours hesitating. The editors of *L'Union* desired to make an appeal to arms, covering the whole ground of the various objections." Houzeau to N. C. Schmit, July 4, 1863, in Correspondance Houzeau-Schmit. Houzeau later claimed to have secretly written other important statements issued by various organizations. In May, 1866, for example, he wrote home: "In the Proceedings of the Convention of the Republican Party of Louisiana, the declaration of principles signed O. J. Dunn, p. 4 and 5, is all entirely mine, without a word changed. The brochure on the Freedmen's Aid Association is entirely mine from beginning to end." Houzeau to his parents, May 6, 1866, in Houzeau Papers.

influence over the whole colored population and bring them into closer contact with government, public affairs, and society in general." On July 9 *L'Union* appeared in both French and English.[28]

When Houzeau left New Orleans for the libraries of Philadelphia in July, 1863, he remained a regular contributor to *L'Union* under the title of "Northern Correspondent." His articles focused primarily on political and military affairs and, according to Houzeau, "created in the colored population of New Orleans an influence that seems positive." He spent one day a week on his correspondence, for which he was paid three thousand francs a year. This arrangement satisfied Houzeau; indeed, in November, 1863, he reassured his mother that, with the exception of local financiers, he was "the happiest man in Philadelphia."[29]

L'Union halted publication on July 19, 1864, bitterly attributing its collapse to the poverty, timidity, and apathy of potential subscribers; the opposition of pro-Confederate Catholic priests; and

28. Houzeau to his parents, July 24, 1863, Houzeau to N. C. Schmit, July 28, 1863 (copy), both in Houzeau Papers.

29. Houzeau to his parents, July 24, 1863, Houzeau to J.-B.-J. Liagre, November 2, 1864 (copy), Houzeau to his mother, November 11, 1863, all in *ibid*. In the November 11 letter to his mother, Houzeau tried to calm her fears that there was "something missing" in his life. He recognized that his family wished he had more "ambition," and he readily admitted that the path he had taken was "much easier (and much easier to accept) than to chase after bigger and better things, which one no doubt can attain from time to time, but having attained them one always desires, by virtue of the same needs, to have something bigger and better yet, always going from desire to desire, from struggle to struggle, without having the time to enjoy what one has attained. . . . Driven a bit by circumstances, and much more perhaps by my native disposition, I know how to live modestly, content with what I have. I would wish that those who worry about me could feel the contentment as I do. What more could I wish for? I refused to be decorated, first of all out of principle, but also because it would have looked like I was getting something, while in my own eyes and given my position, I would not have felt I got anything. It would have been as if the emperor of Turkey had sent me a green turban. I refused a chair at the University of Brussels because I did not feel the personal satisfaction that another might have felt at this offer. And I am ready to refuse again. Like the figure in the Greek legend, what better proof can I give that I am happy with my lot."

the indifference of Union soldiers. Just two days after *L'Union* folded, the New Orleans *Tribune* made its debut. The new paper, which was also edited by Paul Trévigne, announced that it would appear three times a week in both English and French and that it would be published daily upon the arrival of a new press ordered from New York. On October 4 the *Tribune* began publishing every day except Monday. It thus became the first Negro daily in America.[30]

The proprietors of the *Tribune* continued to publish Houzeau's correspondence and in October, 1864, asked him to become the paper's managing editor. Houzeau was moved by the "urgent and sympathetic letters" from these "gentlemen" who "have absolute confidence in me, though they have not known me very long." He was concerned, however, about how his "inner taste for order" and "regularity" would be accepted at the *Tribune*. Moreover, he recognized that the *Tribune* was "expressly the organ of the free colored population" and that he, consequently, would be "only an adviser" and would "not personify it in any way." Troubled even more by the prospect of remaining indefinitely in the United States, he warned the proprietors that his removal to New Orleans would be expensive and that his stay there "might be of short duration." The proprietors, apparently determined to hire Houzeau despite the uncertainty of his commitment, immediately wired him five hundred francs for the trip to New Orleans. After "some hesitation," Houzeau accepted the offer, explaining to a

30. *L'Union*, May 31, 1864; *Tribune*, July 21, September 27, 1864, September 6, 1865 (French ed.). Numerous mistakes exist in the literature concerning the publication of the *Tribune*. For example, Houzeau, "My Passage," 79, errs in stating that the *Tribune* was founded as a French-language paper (it was bilingual from the outset, as he later notes in *ibid.*, 80); McCrary, *Abraham Lincoln*, 387, errs in stating that the *Tribune* was initially published as a weekly (it began as a tri-weekly); and McPherson, *Negro's Civil War*, 346, errs in stating that the file of the *Tribune* is complete in both languages (there are several important gaps, especially those surrounding the riot of July, 1866, and the state elections of April, 1868).

friend that "I would have been crazy to refuse, especially since I am not tied to them for any fixed amount of time; I remain free." He arrived in New Orleans on November 14; eight days later he wrote to his mother: "I have under my charge the press of the colored population."[31]

Although the proprietors knew that Houzeau was white, this fact never made its way into the columns of the *Tribune*. Indeed, the paper declared that it was "edited by men of color" and that it would never be "controlled by any white man." For his part, Houzeau did nothing to dispel the notion that he was a Negro. He enjoyed passing himself off as a man of color and working "with these pariahs of the proslavery society." Even a congressional committee that conducted extensive public and private interviews with him while investigating the New Orleans Riot of 1866 listed him as "colored" in its final report.[32] Subsequent investigators, including a host of talented historians, have also usually assumed that the editor of the New Orleans *Tribune* was black.[33]

31. Houzeau to his father, October 18, 1864, Houzeau to his mother, November 22, 1864, both in Houzeau Papers; Houzeau to J.-B.-J. Liagre, November 2, 1864, in Liagre Papers.
32. *Tribune*, September 10, 1865 (French ed.), September 6, 1864; Houzeau, "My Passage," 75; *House Reports*, 39th Cong., 2nd Sess., No. 16, *Report of the Select Committee on the New Orleans Riots* (1867) (cited hereinafter as *New Orleans Riots*), 73. The same committee listed the free Negroes Lucien Jean Pierre Capla, Jean Baptiste Jourdain, and Eugène Staès as "colored slightly," "slightly colored," and white. *New Orleans Riots*, 119, 204, 118.
33. See, for example, John R. Ficklen, *History of Reconstruction in Louisiana (Through 1868)* (Baltimore, 1910), 188; W. E. Burghardt Du Bois, *Black Reconstruction in America . . . 1860–1880* (New York, 1935), 456; Charles B. Roussève, *The Negro in Louisiana: Aspects of His History and His Literature* (New Orleans, 1937), 119, 125; Roger W. Shugg, *Origins of Class Struggle in Louisiana: A Social History of White Farmers and Laborers During Slavery and After, 1840–1875* (Baton Rouge, 1939), 215; McPherson, *Negro's Civil War*, 129, 269; William S. McFeely, *Yankee Stepfather: General O. O. Howard and the Freedmen* (New Haven, 1968), 166, 333; Roger A. Fischer, *The Segregation Struggle in Louisiana, 1862–77* (Urbana, Ill., 1974), 29; Joe Gray Taylor, *Louisiana Reconstructed, 1863–1877* (Baton Rouge, 1974), 53; William F. Messner, *Freedmen and the Ideology of Free Labor: Louisiana, 1862–1865* (La-

Houzeau admired the men of the *Tribune* for "living very nobly and making many sacrifices to ease the transformation of slaves into freemen." He was particularly impressed with Dr. Louis Charles Roudanez, the *Tribune*'s founder and principal financier.[34]

---

fayette, La., 1978), 109; Leon F. Litwack, *Been in the Storm So Long: The Aftermath of Slavery* (New York, 1979), 509, 512.

Even historians who know that Houzeau edited the *Tribune* have often erred in describing him. Vincent, *Black Legislators*, 25, argues that "a black man, Charles Dallas [*sic*], a native of Texas," and Houzeau were two different people, but in fact Charles J. Dalloz was one of Houzeau's pseudonyms; Connor, "Reconstruction Rebels," 162, 179, misspells Houzeau's family name and has him attending the wrong university and dying in the wrong year; Tinker, *Creole City*, 107, Leavens, "*L'Union*," 23–24, and Rankin, "Politics of Caste," 132, incorrectly assign Houzeau membership in the Institut de France. Pierre Berthon, Archivist of the Académie des Sciences de l'Institut de France, to the editor, September 9, 1980. It should be noted that Houzeau was not the only Caucasian working at the *Tribune*. In late 1865 nearly a quarter of the paper's employees were white. Houzeau to his parents, November 15, 1865, in Houzeau Papers.

34. Houzeau to Victor Bouvy, November 18, 1864, in Liagre Papers. It is clear from the reflections of Paul Trévigne and the letters of Houzeau that Roudanez, who sank over $30,000 in the *Tribune*, was the dominant force behind the paper. Houzeau wrote to J.-B.-J. Liagre on November 2, 1864, that "the president and principal stockholder of the [New Orleans *Tribune*] Corporation is a mulatto doctor, who studied in Europe, and who has his diploma from the [medical] faculty of Paris." In Liagre Papers. Roudanez was assisted, however, by his brother Jean Baptiste, who served as publisher of the *Tribune*. Relatively little is known about Jean Baptiste Roudanez, and historians have revealed some confusion about him. For example, Taylor, *Louisiana Reconstructed*, 135, refers to him as "Dr. Joseph B. Roudanez"; C. Peter Ripley, *Slaves and Freedmen in Civil War Louisiana* (Baton Rouge, 1976), 175, refers to him as "J. B. Roudenez [*sic*], influential editor of the *Tribune*"; Howard A. White, *The Freedmen's Bureau in Louisiana* (Baton Rouge, 1970), 31, 156, suggests he was from Saint Domingue; Tinker, "Bibliography of the French Newspapers," 321, says he was Louis Charles Roudanez's son; Messner, *Freedmen and the Ideology of Free Labor*, 109–10, attributes to him editorials he never wrote; and McPherson, *Negro's Civil War*, 280, attributes to him a speech he never made. Jean Baptiste Roudanez was born in New Orleans in 1815 and died in 1895. Prior to the war he was an engineer and often worked on sugar plantations. During Reconstruction he served as vice-president of the New Orleans Freedmen's Aid Association. In March, 1864, he and E. Arnold Bertonneau delivered a petition to Abraham Lincoln asking that the right to vote be extended to the free colored population of Louisiana. See Trévigne's 1890 reflection on the origins of the *Tribune* in Roussève, *Negro in Louisiana*, 114, 119; Houzeau to J.-B.-J. Liagre, November 2, 1864, in Liagre Papers; *Republican*, March 4, 1868; *Tribune*, April 13, 1864; *Daily*

Louis Charles Roudanez. Reprinted from Rodolphe Lucien Desdunes, *Nos hommes et notre histoire* (Montreal, 1911).

Roudanez was born on June 12, 1823, in St. James Parish, the son of Louis Roudanez, a "very honorable French merchant," and Aimée Potens, a free woman of color. He was baptised a Catholic by the president of the College of New Orleans. His godfather, Marius St. Colomb Bringier, came from an old and distinguished white Louisiana family, and Roudanez himself was recorded as white at the time of his baptism. As a youth he was sent to school in New Orleans and then to France, where he received a bachelor of letters in 1847, a bachelor of sciences in 1849, and a doctorate in medicine in 1853. Roudanez received his medical education at the prestigious Faculté de Médecine de Paris, and his teachers included such luminaries as Auguste Nélaton, Léon Rostan, Armand Velpeau, Jean Baptiste Bouillaud, and Philippe Ricord.[35]

Attending medical school in Paris guaranteed that Roudanez would not only receive the finest training available anywhere in the world but would also become a member of one of the most politically liberal professions in France. Physicians emerged as a liberal force in French politics after the Revolution of 1789 when François Lanthenas challenged his colleagues: "Who, then, should denounce tyrants to mankind if not the doctors, who make man their sole study, and who, each day, . . . contemplate the human miseries that have no other origin but tyranny and slavery?" By

---

Picayune, December 2, 1895; Boston Liberator, April 15, 1864; James McKaye, The Mastership and Its Fruits: The Emancipated Slave Face to Face with His Old Master (New York, 1864), 5; David C. Rankin, "The Origins of Negro Leadership in New Orleans During Reconstruction," in Howard N. Rabinowitz (ed.), Southern Black Leaders of the Reconstruction Era (Urbana, Ill., 1982), 170, 187.

35. St. Michael's Church, Record Book of Baptisms (1823), p. 113, in Archives of the Diocese of Baton Rouge, Baton Rouge, La.; L'Abeille, March 13, 1890; Daily Picayune, March 12, 1890; Faculté de Médecine de Paris, Louis Charles Roudanez transcript, in Archives, Université René Descartes, Paris, France; Louis Charles Roudanez, "De l'endocardite" (M.D. thesis, Faculté de Médecine de Paris, 1853). Although Roudanez and his family repeatedly gave 1826 as the year of his birth, his baptismal registration says that he was born in 1823.

the time of the Revolution of 1848, according to Jules Guérin, editor of the most popular medical journal in France, the entire medical profession was "essentially liberal and republican." While not applicable to all physicians, particularly those living in rural areas, Guérin's characterization aptly describes Ricord and Bouillaud, Roudanez's two favorite teachers. Ricord, a member of the Academy of Medicine and, after Alexandre Dumas, the most decorated celebrity in nineteenth-century France, was a brilliant orator who in 1848 supported the radical proposition that students ought to elect the dean of the Faculté de Médecine. Also a member of the Academy of Medicine, Bouillaud was an outspoken champion of the Revolution of 1848 who owed his position as dean of the Faculté de Médecine to his close friendship with the radical republicans Louis Blanc, Hippolyte Carnot, and Alexandre Ledru-Rollin. These two physicians made a profound impression upon Roudanez, and he began his doctoral thesis by thanking them for their "unusual kindness" as well as their "scholarly courses."[36]

Unlike many other foreign students who came to Paris and then stayed in order to avoid political oppression at home, Roudanez returned to America after finishing his degree. But before settling permanently in New Orleans, he went to New Hampshire where he enrolled in Dartmouth College and received a second medical degree in 1857. It was not without reason, then, that

36. On the medical profession in nineteenth-century France, see Michel Foucault, *The Birth of the Clinic: An Archaeology of Medical Perception*, trans. A. M. Sheridan Smith (New York, 1973), where Lanthenas is quoted on p. 35; Jacques Leonard, *Les médecins de l'Ouest au XIXème siècle* (3 vols.; Paris, 1978), where Guérin is quoted in III, 1231; Erwin H. Ackerknecht, *Medicine at the Paris Hospital, 1794–1848* (Baltimore, 1967); Theodore Zeldin, *France, 1848–1945* (2 vols.; Oxford, 1973, 1977), I, ch. 2. Roudanez served as an aide to Ricord at his Hôpital des Vénériens du Midi, and for his thesis Roudanez chose a topic on which Bouillaud was one of the foremost authorities in the world. Bouillaud was also the physician upon whom Balzac based the lovable Dr. Bianchon in *Comédie humaine*. Houzeau to his father, October 23, 1867, in Houzeau Papers; Ackerknecht, *Medicine*, 110.

29
Introduction

Houzeau described Roudanez as "a mulatto far above the crowd."
He was also, according to Houzeau, a "very close" friend who
took "care of me with the zeal of a brother."[37]

With Roudanez's backing, Houzeau assembled at the *Tribune*
an extraordinary group of black, brown, and white workers. Trévigne, a quadroon who was born in New Orleans of a Spanish
father, was of course already on the scene, and Houzeau found him
an "extremely agreeable" colleague. J. Clovis Laizer, Houzeau's
first appointment to the paper's English edition and the son of
a free woman of color and a Swiss immigrant, was a seasoned
newspaperman who could speak French, Spanish, and English.
When Laizer died unexpectedly in 1869, Houzeau called it "a
great loss for the men of color, the worst." Also trilingual was a
Frenchman from the South of France who gave Houzeau "good
service" after joining the *Tribune* in 1865. Other employees included a young mulatto who ran the night shift, a light-colored
man who had studied at the Lycée Louis le Grand in Paris, a man
whom Houzeau described as "a black with very frizzy hair," and a
number of printers who had served as officers in the Union army.[38]

Publicly, Houzeau praised all his workers for their "effort, devotion, and energy." His private correspondence reveals, how-

37. Louis Charles Roudanez, "De l'accouchement dans la présentation de
l'épaule" (M.D. thesis, Dartmouth College, 1856); *A Catalogue of the Officers and
Students of Dartmouth College, for the Academical Year 1856–7* (Hanover, N.H., 1856),
ix; Records of the Annual Meeting of the Board of Trustees of Dartmouth College,
July, 1857, in Dartmouth College Archives, Dartmouth College, Hanover, N.H.;
Houzeau to his parents, January 18, September 8, 1865, Houzeau to his father, October 23, 1867, all in Houzeau Papers. Houzeau was not the only one impressed
by Roudanez's medical training. Roudanez had a large and lucrative practice, and
at the time of his death in 1890 his open accounts alone consisted of several hundred patients. See the copy of Roudanez's open accounts book in the Succession of
Louis Charles Roudanez (no. 29729), Civil District Court, in New Orleans City
Archives Collection, Louisiana Division, New Orleans Public Library.
38. Rankin, "Origins of Negro Leadership," 188; Houzeau to his parents,
July 23, 1865, May 22, 1869, November 15, 1865, January 15, 1867, June 17, 1866,
all in Houzeau Papers.

ever, that he had some reservations about his employees. He was distressed that at first his staff bickered constantly, that some of his employees knew only one language, and that all of them repeated confidential conversations. More generally, he wrote in 1867 that "the great difficulty for me has always been to find some 'lieutenants' who are educated and devoted at the same time. I have not found a single white who knows how to think like a black. All of them that I have tried ended up being false without perceiving it. As for the mulattoes, they lack education and energy for work." This last theme was not a new one for Houzeau; in 1866 he had complained that the colored Creoles "are well intentioned, impassioned at times, but subdued when the enthusiasm has abated; they are not sorry to find the work all done and to take the credit for it."[39]

Houzeau himself was a tireless worker who realized that "an immense amount of work is required to make Freedom a substantial boon." He devoted virtually every waking moment to the *Tribune*, and he expected the same kind of total commitment from his employees. On a typical day he got up at five thirty and had breakfast. By six o'clock he was at his desk writing two different editorials, one in English and one in French. By ten he was finished and had a second breakfast. He then walked a half mile from

39. Houzeau, "My Passage," 148; Houzeau to his mother, November 15, 1865, Houzeau to his parents, June 17, May 6, 1866, March 31, 1867, all in Houzeau Papers; Houzeau to Victor Bouvy, January 6, 1867, in Liagre Papers. In the letter to his mother of November 15, 1865, Houzeau wrote: "When I first came [back to the *Tribune* as editor], the foremen were quarreling with the workers, the workers quarreling among themselves, and the office personnel constantly flaring up at their subordinates. People were shouting, swearing, and I believe they were even coming to blows sometimes." According to Houzeau, things improved dramatically under his direction, but he still complained in February, 1866, that "it is extremely depressing that I have no one whom I don't have to watch over; but that's the way it is. It is due to this principle I have of 'never giving an order without making sure it is carried out' that I have been able to make something out of this press." Houzeau to his parents, February 18, 1866, in Houzeau Papers.

his apartment on Canal Street to the *Tribune* office in the French Quarter.[40] There he assigned tasks to the day shift and began a series of "excessively tedious" appointments with special pleaders who ranged from steamboatmen to state legislators. At three o'clock he went to dinner, which was always hurried because he had to get back to the press. At five thirty he distributed the work for the night shift and read proofs. During the evening he covered various political and philanthropic meetings until nine or ten o'clock. He then returned to the press and read proofs until midnight. During the week following the New Orleans Riot of July, 1866, Houzeau worked even longer days and almost single-handedly put out the *Tribune*. By November, 1866, he had written 1,500 articles for the paper. A few months later he complained that he was utterly exhausted and that the last two and a half years of his life seemed like five.[41]

40. Houzeau to N. C. Schmit, May 28, 1865, in Correspondance Houzeau-Schmit; Houzeau to his mother, November 15, 1865, in Houzeau Papers. Houzeau is listed as a white "printer" living at 245 Canal Street in *Gardner's New Orleans Directory for 1867* . . . (New Orleans, 1867), 207. He took the "precaution" of living on Canal Street when he first joined the *Tribune* because it was "the safest in the city." He nevertheless lived in fear of harassment by Confederate sympathizers. He gave up the theater because he was afraid that if he attended there would be "some provocation made against me"; he even resorted to addressing his parents as "My Dear Friends" in his letters home because he suspected that his correspondence was being monitored. In the summer of 1867 he moved to a house in the suburbs that was about six miles from the *Tribune* office. Houzeau to his parents, August 26, 1866, January 18, 1865, July 4, 1867, all in Houzeau Papers; *New Orleans Riots*, 75. The *Tribune* was always based in the French Quarter, though not at the same address. It was at 21 Conti Street from July 21, 1864, through November 24, 1866; thereafter it was at 122 and 124 Exchange Alley.

41. Houzeau wrote of the special pleaders: "If I work with pleasure for the cause of progress in general, I cannot find an equal enthusiasm and interest in the personal affairs of so many people whom I did not know before and do not care to know once I have met them. I believe that there are more boorish intruders here than anywhere else on earth, and that on this particular point New Orleans could give lessons to Paris." Houzeau to his mother, November 15, 1865, in Houzeau Papers. On Houzeau's work routine and fatigue, see Houzeau to his mother, November 15, 1865, November 18, 1866, Houzeau to his brother Auguste, August 5, 1866, Houzeau to his parents, March 31, 1867, all in *ibid*.

OFFICE OF NEW ORLEANS TRIBUNE,
122 and 124 EXCHANGE ALLEY.

N° 36 C.

New Orleans, 29 octobre 1867.

Mes chers parents,

Je vous ai écrit le 23, en vous promettant
de vous donner sous peu de mes nouvelles,
afin de vous rassurer entièrement sur
ma santé. Je viens m'acquitter de cette
promesse, et vous annoncer que j'ai
repris toutes mes habitudes et que je
suis parfaitement rétabli. J'ai recouvré
toutes mes forces, et ne songe plus à
l'indisposition que j'ai eue, sinon pour
m'applaudir d'être acclimaté à si bon
marché.

Je ne suis pas encore décidé si je resterai
pour l'hiver dans mon faubourg; beaucoup
de personnes me conseillent de revenir en
ville; mais je suis déjà si habitué à la

Autograph letter from Houzeau to his parents. Courtesy of Service
Photographique, Bibliothèque Royale Albert Ier, Brussels.

Houzeau devoted much of his energy at the *Tribune* to two in-
terrelated goals: improving and emphasizing the paper's English
edition, and increasing the paper's influence. He, of course, realized the importance of the French edition. After all, the vast majority of the *Tribune*'s subscribers were French-speaking free coloreds. Moreover, the French edition could be used to rally support
in Europe, and in fact Victor Hugo, Louis Blanc, Jules Michelet,
Edgar Quinet, Victor Schoelcher, Armand Barbès, Adolphe Cré-
mieux, and other prominent Frenchmen did contribute to such
Tribune-backed organizations as the New Orleans Freedmen's Aid
Association. But Houzeau also realized that free coloreds and liberal Europeans formed a tiny and powerless constituency, and he
had no illusion that support would be forthcoming from the
French-speaking whites of southern Louisiana. Indeed, Houzeau
found the white Creoles pretentious, dishonest, dissolute, racist,
and reactionary.[42] To be influential in America, Houzeau reasoned,
the *Tribune*'s English edition would have to take priority over its
French edition and would have to reach English-speaking blacks
and whites residing not only in Louisiana but throughout the na-

42. Houzeau, "My Passage," 79–83; *Tribune*, May 8, 1866; Houzeau to his parents, July 22, 1866, in Houzeau Papers. It is impossible to exaggerate Houzeau's
contempt for the white Creoles. In the letter of July 22, 1866, he wrote that "the
European quarter of New Orleans is a disgrace for a civilized city. This is the quarter where they speak French and Spanish. The American city has an immense contempt for this old area, and it seems to me pretty much merited. Reigning there are
Latin customs, reinforced with all the libertinage that these customs acquire when
practiced in a distant, foreign, and free land. What a contrast with the severity of
the Anglo-Saxons, who are without doubt cold, but who control themselves. With
a very small number of exceptions, this Latin society of New Orleans is not an
honorable society—neither the men nor the women—from any point of view. I
am not easily scandalized, but I constantly say to myself: how can such a race, such
a people, have the pretention to colonize and dominate others? Here one naturally
finds the most cruel and rabid slaveholders—people who are never truthful nor
practical. Great luxury, sumptuous clothing, debts up to their ears, all sorts of par-
ties at night, drunkenness, swindling without shame when you have a business
affair with them. The most virtuous women—I'm speaking of the cream of the
crop—are those who have had syphilis only five times."

tion. By early 1866 the paper contended that "there is not a single colored man who does not feel that the *Tribune* is the rostrum from which the oppressed and the down-trodden may be heard by the American nation." To guarantee that white Americans, especially those with political clout, also heard the *Tribune*, Houzeau instructed his staff to send hundreds of copies of the paper to members of Congress and other important public officials. "From this day forward," Houzeau wrote on July 24, 1865, to General Oliver O. Howard, commissioner of the Freedmen's Bureau, "the N. O. *Tribune* will be sent to you. I take the liberty to state that the *Tribune* takes a particular interest in the welfare of the freedmen, and is the only paper in Louisiana that exposes the wrongs perpetrated against them."[43]

Under Houzeau's direction the *Tribune* did pay particular attention to the condition of the freedmen, thereby adopting a position significantly different from that of *L'Union*. To be sure, *L'Union* had championed the abolition of slavery, but the paper was above all concerned with the special interests of the free colored caste, which was predominantly middle class, French speaking, light colored, free born, and Catholic. Indeed, *L'Union* feared that the crusade against slavery might totally eclipse the free colored campaign for political equality. Thus, on April 11, 1863, *L'Union* praised Louisiana Unionists for demanding the abolition of slav-

43. *Tribune*, February 1, 1866; Houzeau to his parents, February 18, 1866, in Houzeau Papers; Ch. J. Dalloz [Houzeau] to O. O. Howard, July 24, 1865, in Oliver O. Howard Papers, Bowdoin College, Brunswick, Maine. Houzeau adopted the name Charles J. Dalloz when he sailed from Mexico to New Orleans in early 1863, and he continued to use it while editor of the *Tribune*. "Charles J. Dalloz" is listed as the "Editor" of the New Orleans *Tribune* in *Louisiana State Gazetteer and Business Man's Guide, for 1866 and 1867* (New Orleans, n.d.), 167. Lancaster, "J.-C. Houzeau," liv*n*; Houzeau to his parents, October 10, 1866, in Houzeau Papers; Houzeau to N. C. Schmit, May 28, 1867, in Correspondance Houzeau-Schmit; *New Orleans Riots*, 73, where Houzeau's pseudonym is incorrectly spelled "Charles Dallas."

ery at numerous rallies, but it simultaneously expressed its dismay "that not one voice from the midst of these assemblies had
been lifted to plead in favor of our rights." Nearly a year later
L'Union declared its hope that someday there would be no invid-
ious distinctions among different groups of people. In the mean-
time the paper voiced its resentment that the free coloreds—"a
class which by its industry and education possesses all the qualifications necessary to exercise the right of suffrage in an intelligent
manner"—were disfranchised because legally they belonged to
the same race as the freedmen. "All those who . . . have lived in
New Orleans long enough to be familiar with the [free] colored
population of this city and appreciate its worth," the paper was
confident, "are in favor of endowing this population with the elective franchise." And throughout its existence *L'Union* had made it
clear that "this population" did not include ex-slaves, the vast
majority of whom were poor, black, illiterate, unskilled, English
speaking, and Protestant.[44]

Initially, the *Tribune* itself displayed some of the same caste
pretentions that had plagued *L'Union*. On July 28, 1864, for instance, the *Tribune* denounced the new state constitution for only
freeing the slaves and not also "granting, through the Constitution itself, the right of suffrage to another portion of the most
loyal citizens of the United States—which would not be a favor,
but an act of justice." A week later, in language almost identical to
that employed by *L'Union* six months earlier, the *Tribune* com-

44. *L'Union*, February 11, 1864. *L'Union* was also committed to the cause of
the Union, perhaps too committed from the perspective of Louisiana slaves. Certainly, the latter were not overjoyed by the paper's decision to fly Lincoln's words,
"l'Union avec des esclaves, l'Union sans esclaves,—l'Union quand même," at the
masthead of its inaugural edition or by the paper's subsequent contention that "the
real question" raised by the Civil War was not the "question of the freedom or
slavery of any class of our inhabitants" but the "vital republican principle" of majority rule. *L'Union*, September 27, 1862, July 9, 1863.

plained that "while we are of the same race as the unfortunate sons of Africa who have trembled until now under the bondage of a cruel and brutalizing slavery, one cannot, without being unfair, confuse the newly freed people with our intelligent population." Even after Houzeau's arrival the French edition of the *Tribune* plaintively reminded its free colored readers that whereas "your slave brothers have gained liberty, and have been made your equals," the colored Creoles had been left "in the shadow and in oblivion." "From the political point of view," the paper asked, "what right has it [the free colored population] obtained? It has nothing more than it had fifty years ago."[45]

Houzeau realized that such divisive rhetoric would make it impossible for the *Tribune* to be the driving and unifying force he envisioned when he wrote that "these people have to be made to agree with one another, given confidence in themselves by means of the newspaper, driven to demand their rights, and this in the midst of all sorts of intrigues and all kinds of opposition." Gradually, though, the *Tribune* expunged from its pages the most flagrant examples of caste consciousness and, through a series of articles that often mixed pragmatism with paternalism, demanded the enfranchisement of both free and freed Negroes.[46]

The *Tribune* may have deemed suffrage "the dearest of our aspirations," but its demands did not stop there. The paper also claimed for all Negroes the right to serve on juries, to ride in nonsegregated streetcars, to attend integrated schools, and to enjoy public places such as theaters and restaurants without discrimination. The paper further maintained that the freedmen had the right to control their own labor and make a decent living. Even before Houzeau's arrival the paper had denounced the "free la-

45. *Tribune*, August 4, 1864 (French ed.), January 8, 1865 (French ed.).
46. Houzeau to his parents, May 6, 1866, in Houzeau Papers. For a more detailed discussion of *L'Union*, the *Tribune*, and the question of Negro suffrage, see Rankin, "Politics of Caste," 125–38.

bor" system introduced by Nathaniel P. Banks, commanding general of the Department of the Gulf from late 1862 until mid-1864, as a disastrous failure where "the plantations were leased out to avaricious adventurers from the North, whose sole desire was to *exploit* the services of the freedmen. . . . The slaves were made serfs and chained to the soil." After Houzeau assumed the editorship and it became increasingly clear that white southerners would be allowed to reclaim their plantations, the *Tribune* protested: "Can a planter be expected to treat the laborers under his control in any other way to-day than he has treated them for the last twenty years? He and they are the same men, in the same place, bearing to each other, in all respects, the same apparent relations. No visible change has passed off between them. The Proclamation of Emancipation did not invest the slave with a physical sign of freedom. It was an all metaphysical endowment."[47]

The solution, the *Tribune* contended, was to "let the land go into the hands of actual laborers," for one cannot expect "complete and perfect freedom for the working men, so long as they remain the tools of capital, and are deprived of the legitimate product of the sweat of their brow." There was, according to the paper, "no more room, in the organization of our society, for an oligarchy of slaveholders, or property holders." The planter class would be replaced by the mass of workers who, since "capital is created by labor," would themselves raise the capital to operate the plantations. The freedmen would purchase small shares in "self-help" banks, which would in turn buy land and factories and rent them to voluntary associations of workers. A portion of the profits from each enterprise would be returned to the banks to expand their ownership of land and factories, and the rest would be divided among the workers.[48]

47. *Tribune*, December 7, September 10, 1864, July 16, 1865.
48. *Ibid.*, July 16, March 8, 1, 1865. The banks, according to the *Tribune* of February 28, 1865, would substitute for "the aristocratic planters the whole power of

In formulating this radical economic program, Houzeau drew upon a variety of European theorists, including the French utopian Charles Fourier and the German reformer Franz Hermann Schulze-Delitzsch. He also borrowed ideas from local white activists such as Benjamin F. Flanders, whom the *Tribune* described in 1864 as "well known in this State and abroad for his devotion to the interest of the Freedmen and the working classes generally," and Charles W. Hornor, a lawyer from Philadelphia who, as secretary of the New Orleans Freedmen's Aid Association, warned in 1865 that following the abolition of slavery the planters would "strive to devise some new system of labor—a system by which the laborers will become mere serfs of capital." Houzeau was most influenced, however, by Hornor's law partner, Thomas Jefferson Durant. A utopian socialist who insisted that his friends be unpretentious "plain folks like myself," Durant had since the mid-1840s deplored the "morality of competitive commerce" and called for a society that would "apply the laws of love and charity to the social relations of men." In 1863 he declared that the real purpose of secession was to destroy "the liberty of the working classes" and to establish "a government in which labor should belong to capital, without regard to color." Two years later he held that liberty extended to the freedmen not only "the right to work" but also "the right to own the soil that he tills"; that "the colored people, as a whole, are as fit, intellectually, as the white men"; and that "the question [of Negro suffrage] is not between black and white,

our people. After having proclaimed the liberty of the workmen, we now have to democratize the capital in their hands." Earlier the *Tribune* and *L'Union* had encouraged the federal government to confiscate the South's plantations, divide them into small farms, and distribute them "among those persons who had, by dint of daily and long continued toil, created all the wealth of the South. Common justice between man and man demanded this step, as some slight recompense for unrequited labor and all the sufferings endured from generation to generation." *Tribune*, September 10, 1864, August 31, 1865; Connor, "Reconstruction Rebels," 170–77.

but between capital and labor. Is it best that the capitalist owns its labor? Or is it best that, as the Constitution intended to have it, the laborer be the political equal of the capitalist." Houzeau, needless to say, exhibited a deep affection for Durant and his ideas.[49]

Under Houzeau's direction the *Tribune* flourished. The paper hinted at its prosperity in 1865: "How far we have been successful, it is not for us to decide; but public sympathy and the liberal patronage conferred upon the TRIBUNE have been a reward for our efforts and an inducement to extend the usefulness of our paper." It claimed to have an audience among "the most active" freedmen in rural Louisiana and "a better circulation than any other paper in the city [of New Orleans]." The latter boast is doubtful, but pro-*Tribune* organizations did all they could to stimulate sales. The National Equal Rights League, for instance, passed a resolution at its Louisiana convention declaring "that it is the duty of each and every league in the State to subscribe to said Journal and extend its circulation among the oppressed." The paper also achieved a considerable following in Washington, D.C., among congressmen such as Charles Sumner, William Kelley, George Julian, Lyman Trumbull, and Richard Yates. Indeed, when Senator Henry Wilson visited New Orleans during Reconstruction, his

49. Connor, "Reconstruction Rebels," 170–77; *Tribune*, October 30, 1864, May 2, June 18, December 24, February 4, 1865; Durant to his mother, January 3, 1846, Durant to Henry O. Ames, December 28, 1845, in Thomas J. Durant Papers, New-York Historical Society, New York, N.Y.; *Times*, November 15, 1863, quoted in Joseph G. Tregle, Jr., "Thomas J. Durant, Utopian Socialism, and the Failure of Presidential Reconstruction in Louisiana," *Journal of Southern History*, XLV (1979), 507. Durant was proud of his long-standing ties to the free coloreds. Writing in support of their request for the right to vote, he noted in 1863 that "I have had long and intimate business relations with the leading free men of African descent in this city, and believe that I employ their confidence to as great an extent as any other in the city." Durant to Salmon P. Chase, December 4, 1863, in Salmon P. Chase Papers, Manuscript Division, Library of Congress, Washington, D.C. In 1882 when Houzeau returned to the United States on an astronomical expedition, he searched for his old friend Durant, only to learn from Hornor that he was dead. Houzeau to his parents, July 28, 1882, in Houzeau Papers.

first stop was the office of the *Tribune*. The Louisiana correspondent of the New York *Tribune* described the paper as "a good Union paper—the best in New Orleans." Paul Trévigne thought the paper's achievements self-evident. "What good the paper did for the success of the cause, everybody knows," he wrote in 1890. A few years later the free colored historian Rodolphe Desdunes made much the same point and singled out Houzeau for special praise: "A learned man and a friend of the oppressed, he put all his ardor and talents into the service of the cause he embraced." Durant, who believed that Houzeau was essential to the *Tribune*'s success, doubted whether "there is in the United States a newspaper writer that one could compare with him, and I presume that there is hardly anyone his equal in France." [50]

The proprietors of the *Tribune* were equally impressed. Un-

50. *Tribune*, January 21, October 14, 1865, February 10, 1866, January 15, 1865. The *Tribune* repeatedly thanked the offices of the above-mentioned congressmen for sending helpful articles, speeches, correspondence, etc. On Wilson's visit, see Houzeau to his father, August 24, 1872, in Houzeau Papers. The New York *Tribune* correspondent is quoted in *New Orleans Riots*, 485; Trévigne is quoted in Roussève, *Negro in Louisiana*, 114, 119; Rodolphe Lucien Desdunes, *Our People and Our History: A Tribute to the Creole People of Color in Memory of the Great Men They Have Given Us and of the Good Works They Have Accomplished*, trans. and ed. Sister Dorothea Olga McCants (1911; Baton Rouge, 1973), 133; Durant is quoted in Houzeau to his parents, February 7, 1869, but see also Houzeau to his parents, January 24, 1869, both in Houzeau Papers. A more critical evaluation of Houzeau's performance at the *Tribune* may be found in John W. Blassingame, *Black New Orleans, 1860–1880* (Chicago, 1973), 131, who argues that "the character of the paper changed dramatically and for the worse shortly after Jean-Charles Houzeau, a radical Belgian geographer, took over as the *Tribune*'s coeditor." Blassingame seems to rest his critique on the fact that there was less social, literary, and foreign (primarily French and Haitian) news in the *Tribune* after Houzeau's arrival. But it was, of course, precisely because he wanted to de-emphasize this kind of elitist material that was directed to the free colored caste and give fuller attention to the political and economic issues affecting all Negroes that Roudanez hired Houzeau. Blassingame's analysis also suffers from his apparent confusion as to when Houzeau became editor of the *Tribune*. For example, after stating that the paper "changed dramatically and for the worse shortly after Jean-Charles Houzeau . . . took over," Blassingame declares that "for the first two years of its existence, the French- and English-language *Tribune* was one of the most impressive of New Or-

doubtedly, they were at times fed up with Houzeau, for he could be arrogant and condescending. After all, here was a man who regarded his work at the *Tribune* as primarily "a mission of philanthropy"; who named himself "Cham" after the biblical father whose children were slaves and blacks;[51] who found fault with virtually everyone on his staff; and who, shortly after leaving the *Tribune*, complained that the proprietors were squandering "the good reputation that I had made for them and the advantages that I had acquired for them." But the proprietors also recognized that Houzeau was a proven radical, a compulsive worker, and a brilliant propagandist. They did everything in their power to keep him at the *Tribune*. They repeatedly raised his salary, and it climbed from 6,000 francs in 1864 to 14,000 francs by the end of 1866. When he announced his intention to resign in 1867, they summoned him to "an intimate interview" and promised more money, more free time, and a house in the country. "Why, you are 'our adopted brother,'" they told him, "and after having gone through the bad times with us, you cannot leave us on the eve of our triumph. Would you like anything else? Demand it. Leave us only the benefit of your counsel and your ideas." They sought to retain him in 1868 although they at that time disagreed vehemently with his counsel and ideas. They even tried to rehire him after he had emigrated to Jamaica. "The New Orleans *Tribune* is revived," Houzeau wrote to his parents in 1869, ". . . and I have received

---

leans papers." Houzeau was editor of the *Tribune* for slightly more than twenty of its first twenty-four months of existence.

51. Houzeau to Victor Bouvy, November 18, 1864, in Liagre Papers; Houzeau to J.-B.-J. Liagre, November 2, 1864 (copy), in Houzeau Papers; Winthrop D. Jordan, *White Over Black: American Attitudes Toward the Negro, 1550–1812* (Chapel Hill, 1968), 17–20, 36. Houzeau published his first articles in the *Tribune* under the name "Cham." The taking of a biblical name for one of his pseudonyms should not be interpreted as a sign of Houzeau's religiosity. He was an agnostic who forbade even the discussion of religion in his home. Lancaster, "J.-C. Houzeau," cx–cxi.

many letters calling me back with the same advantages that I enjoyed in January 1868."[52]

Houzeau, who did not believe himself "indispensible" to the *Tribune*, attributed his popularity with the proprietors to his "absolute personal independence" and to his compassion for the oppressed. "For myself," he wrote in 1867, "who knew how to make myself a proletarian in Europe, it has not been difficult to make myself black in the United States. I think and I feel that which a freedman must think and feel. I do not consider things from the point of view of a protector, but as they have told me a hundred times, I really am one of them." But even more important than his ability to empathize with the downtrodden, according to Houzeau, was his independence, which came from being a foreigner without political aspirations. "It is," he explained to a Belgian friend, "the absence in me of personal designs which has made my independence, and which has made me 'a sure man,' identified with the cause of the elevation of the black."[53]

Although Belgian citizenship disqualified Houzeau from either voting or holding public office in Louisiana, it clearly did not

52. Houzeau to his parents, May 9, 1868, May 26, 1867, March 2, 1868, January 24, 1869, all in Houzeau Papers; Houzeau to Victor Bouvy, January 6, 1867, in Liagre Papers.

53. Houzeau wrote to his parents on March 31, 1867, that the proprietors of the *Tribune* would hate to lose him as editor, "but I do not have the vanity to believe myself indispensible. They will divide the English and the French [editions]; there will be two heads instead of one; they will hire some good assistants, and then things will march on." A few months earlier Houzeau had explained to his mother why it would "be difficult" to find someone to replace him: "Although there are many who speak the two languages, there are few who can write both French and English—who write them well enough to publish articles and conduct business matters. I have investigated those who have approached me: none are qualified. An American could do the English part better than I could; but the colored population speaks French, and there would be no similarity between him and those he must represent." Houzeau to his mother, November 18, 1866, in Houzeau Papers. On Houzeau's independence, see Houzeau to Victor Bouvy, January 6, May 28, 1867, both in Liagre Papers.

hamper his work for the freedmen. "There remains a lot to be done to help the freed slaves," he wrote his parents in the summer of 1865, "and I don't spare my efforts in their behalf. I am often appointed to serve on committees, and when I am I don't allow useful projects to stagnate. Because others are so lazy, it is often I, a foreigner, who pushes to get things done." He was active in numerous philanthropic organizations, to which he also contributed five or six hundred francs a year. As a member of the board of directors of the New Orleans Freedmen's Aid Association, he worked to help the freedmen set up their own farms; and as vice-president of the Louisiana Homestead Association, he assisted the freedmen in their efforts to obtain land under the Southern Homestead Act of 1866. He helped draft important resolutions calling for Negro rights that were ratified at mass political rallies; he contributed to pamphlets on the freedmen's condition that were sent abroad for the purpose of enlisting moral and financial support; and he made speeches (in French) before groups such as the free colored society that annually celebrated the French government's 1848 edict abolishing slavery and extending the right of citizenship to all men regardless of race. He also held elective posts in both the Friends of Universal Suffrage and the Republican party. Following one such election, Houzeau complained of his "celebrity" and declared that he would prefer "to remain unknown; but my position will not allow me to hide forever."[54]

54. Houzeau to his parents, July 23, 1865, May 6, 1866, March 31, October 3, 1867, all in Houzeau Papers; *Tribune*, April 13, September 19, 1865; Houzeau, "My Passage," 146. While in New Orleans Houzeau also taught himself shorthand so that he could take more accurate and complete notes, and served briefly as a correspondent for the New York *Evening Post*, for which he received 350 francs a month. I have been unable to find any articles in the *Evening Post* under any of Houzeau's known pseudonyms, but I have found a piece entitled "Reconstruction in Louisiana" that reads like something from his pen. Houzeau to N. C. Schmit, April 22, 1866, in Correspondance Houzeau-Schmit; Houzeau to his parents, April 21, 1867, in Houzeau Papers; New York *Evening Post*, April 4, 1867.

Usually, however, Houzeau was able to avoid the limelight and quietly concentrate on formulating the *Tribune*'s response to the major issues raised by Reconstruction in Louisiana. He was disappointed with Lincoln and continued the paper's existing strategy of attacking the president for his "tame, vacillating, halting policy." As implemented in Louisiana by General Banks, Lincoln's plan of Reconstruction was a "complete failure." Its principal achievement, the Constitution of 1864, did virtually nothing to improve the status of Negroes beyond the required abolition of slavery, and it "restored power to the avowed as well as the secret enemies of our beloved Republic." The *Tribune* expected a much tougher stance from Andrew Johnson and initially thought he would effect a "social revolution" throughout the South by confiscating and redistributing massive tracts of land held by the planter class. Before long, however, the paper was castigating Johnson as a treacherous reactionary who might even try to replace slavery with serfdom. Moreover, the new Louisiana government that was elected in November, 1865, was composed almost entirely of Democrats and former rebels. At the state capitol, where the doorkeeper wore a Confederate uniform, members of the legislature set to work passing Black Codes that reduced the freedmen to a status reminiscent of slavery. Incredulous, the *Tribune* responded: "Reconstruction is a phantom, an air-castle, that has no substance and no reality. Reconstruction is still an unsolved problem. Nothing is done yet; all remains to be taken care of by the people—the whole people—and by Congress."[55]

But Congress was also disturbed by what was taking place under Johnson's plan of restoration and by July, 1866, had passed the

55. *Tribune*, September 22, 1864, May 19, 6, 1865, September 11, March 14, 1866; Taylor, *Louisiana Reconstructed*, 73, 80, 99–102. The *Tribune* repeatedly called upon Congress to take charge of Reconstruction in Louisiana, but actually Houzeau did not expect Congress to intervene until all other means of stopping the reestablishment of slavery had been exhausted. Houzeau to N. C. Schmit, December 7, 1865, in Correspondance Houzeau-Schmit.

Civil Rights Act, a bill extending the life of the Freedmen's Bureau, and the Fourteenth Amendment. The *Tribune* applauded Congress' decision to play a more active role in Reconstruction but doubted whether the Civil Rights Act, "so long the hope of the oppressed," would actually have much impact. Commenting on the act after it became law, the *Tribune* observed: "Nothing has been changed, no more regard is paid to-day to our rights than was before, and we have not met with a larger sense of justice than previously." The paper had even stronger reservations about the bill to extend the life and expand the power of the Freedmen's Bureau. "Should the Bureau be withdrawn," the paper charged, "not ten colored men would take notice of it or find anything changed. Planters alone would lose. For the machinery of the Bureau is now used by them to intimidate the uneducated blacks, and to make the most of their contracts." On August 12, 1866, less than a month after Congress decided to prop the bureau up, the *Tribune* advised the nation to "let the Freedmen's Bureau go down."[56] The paper had a higher opinion of the Fourteenth Amendment but complained that it did not possess "all the guarantees that the country had the right and the duty to expect." Particularly distressing was the amendment's second section, which failed to write Negro suffrage unequivocally into the Constitution and instead cleared the way for Negro disfranchisement by leaving the question of voter eligibility in the hands of individual states.[57]

56. *Tribune*, April 29, May 11, 1866. The Freedmen's Bureau was ineffective, the *Tribune* explained, because many of its agents are "imbued with the common prejudices against us," and because "the agents of the Freedmen's Bureau are very few. In most of the parishes there are none. And where there are any, they feel very isolated, and nearly without power to enforce the regulations and obtain redress and justice. In the midst of a hostile population they act cautiously. Their acquaintances are among the whites, and they cannot easily combat the influence of the false impressions and misrepresentations that are conveyed to them every day, and every hour of the day." *Ibid.*, August 31, December 14, 1865.

57. *Ibid.*, October 16 (French ed.), 31 (French ed.), 1866. The *Tribune* feared

A month after Congress adopted the Fourteenth Amendment, a group of Louisiana Republicans reconvened the 1864 state constitutional convention for the purpose of taking the vote away from rebel whites and bestowing it upon loyal Negroes. When an angry white mob attacked the convention on July 30, 1866, the result was the bloodiest riot of the entire Reconstruction era. "It was not a battle," according to Houzeau, who attended the gathering as a reporter for the *Tribune*, "but a frightful massacre." Voters in the North agreed, and in the congressional elections in the fall of 1866 they overwhelmingly elected men who opposed Johnson's lenient plan of restoration. The elections, the *Tribune* contended, were among "the most striking and most encouraging ever put on record" and constituted nothing less than "une révolution dans le Nord." The paper could "now wait with a renewed confidence for the development of the Republican policy." That policy, as eventually outlined in the Reconstruction Act of March 2, 1867, divided the South into five districts under the command of military governors who were to conduct a voter registration, for which Negroes would be eligible, and oversee the election of constitutional conventions, which were required to write Negro suffrage into the new state constitutions. Houzeau was ecstatic. This "victory," he informed his parents, grants "my colored friends . . . possession of the right to vote, which means that the last conquest they had wanted is realized." A year later when the Louisiana constitutional convention, half of whose delegates were Negroes, adopted a document "magnificent for its liberal principles," Houzeau proudly reported that "the Constitution is entirely in our direction." The *Tribune* and its allies had "won all the battles,"

---

that under the Fourteenth Amendment white Republicans as well as white Democrats might exclude Negroes from the franchise. On November 25, 1866, the paper stated its opposition to the disfranchisement of ex-Confederates. If they are denied the vote, the paper reasoned, "then the loyal 'qualified voters' will no longer have an interest in upholding our claims to the right of suffrage."

including the fiercely contested struggle over integrated public schools. Houzeau pronounced the Constitution "an immense success," under which "the future of the colored race is assured, because its rights and its means of development are."[58]

At this moment of triumph, a rift developed between Houzeau and the proprietors of the *Tribune*. "For several weeks," Houzeau wrote on March 2, 1868, "I have found myself at odds with its [the *Tribune*'s] principal proprietors on the real interests of this population, and the political path to take. It was the first serious dispute in three years." The quarrel resulted from the paper's inability to control the 1868 Republican nominating convention, which met in New Orleans in January to choose candidates for the upcoming state elections. At the convention an ambitious group of white northerners succeeded in gaining the party's gubernatorial nomination for Henry Clay Warmoth, a native of Illinois who had come to Louisiana as an officer in the Union army. For his running mate the handsome young carpetbagger picked Oscar James Dunn, a "very black man of color" who, according to a Negro newspaper, bore "the unmistakable marks of the African so prominent[ly] that none need look twice to convince himself that he belongs to the race so lately enfranchised." A former barber who described himself as "comparatively a poor man," Dunn was the English-speaking son of an ex-slave. He and Warmoth were joined on the Republican ticket by other Negroes and northern whites.[59]

The proprietors of the *Tribune*, whose candidate for the guber-

58. Houzeau, "My Passage," 128, 143; *Tribune*, October 12, 14 (French ed.), November 11, 1866; Houzeau to his parents, March 31, 1867, March 2, 1868, both in Houzeau Papers; Houzeau to Victor Bouvy, April 18, 1867, in Liagre Papers; Houzeau to N. C. Schmit, March 2, 1868, in Correspondance Houzeau-Schmit.

59. Houzeau to N. C. Schmit, March 2, 1868, in Correspondance Houzeau-Schmit; *Radical Standard*, February 27, 1869; *House Miscellaneous Documents*, 41st Cong., 2nd Sess., No. 154, *Testimony Taken by the Sub-Committee of Elections in Louisiana* (1870) (cited hereinafter as *Elections in Louisiana*) pt. 1, p. 181.

natorial nomination had lost to Warmoth by two votes, refused to support the Republican ticket and instead asked James Govan Taliaferro to head an independent ticket. Taliaferro, a longtime Unionist who had spent time in a Confederate prison during the Civil War, was a white Louisianian from Catahoula Parish who in 1860 had owned twenty-seven slaves and a plantation valued at $87,000. He had initially opposed ratification of the Thirteenth Amendment and in 1865 had run for lieutenant governor on a platform opposing Negro suffrage. For Taliaferro's running mate, Roudanez and his associates chose the former Union officer Francis Ernest Dumas, an extremely wealthy and almost white free man of color who had also been a large Louisiana slaveholder before the war. Born, reared, and educated in France, Dumas, according to the novelist John W. De Forest, could "speak good French, but nothing else." Roudanez distributed the remaining places on his ticket to Negroes and southern whites.[60]

Houzeau found Roudanez's strategy in supporting the Taliaferro-Dumas ticket "neither wise, nor logical, nor liberal." To be sure, he understood why "the so-called French colored element, the Franco-Africans," despised Warmoth and the other "Yankee adventurers arriving in the baggage of the federal army," for they were a shameless lot who "regarded the colored race as a simple instrument . . . for profit and advancement." Nevertheless,

60. *Republican*, March 29, 1868; Wynona G. Mills, "James Govan Taliaferro (1798–1876): Louisiana Unionist and Scalawag" (M.A. thesis, Louisiana State University, 1968), 1–52; Francis E. Dumas Pension, Records of the Veterans Administration, in Record Group 15, National Archives; *Tribune*, July 2, 1867; John W. De Forest, *A Volunteer's Adventures: A Union Captain's Record of the Civil War*, ed. James H. Croushore (London, 1946), 47–48. Dumas, the *Tribune's* candidate for governor at the Republican nominating convention of January 13–14, had, after losing the nomination to Warmoth, been offered the party's nomination for lieutenant governor "in the spirit of conciliation and kindness." Dumas refused the offer. Warmoth charged that the *Tribune* "forced" Dumas "to decline our nomination." *Republican*, March 29, 1868; Henry Clay Warmoth, *War, Politics and Reconstruction: Stormy Days in Louisiana* (New York, 1930), 58.

49
Introduction

Houzeau argued, "the war cry against the Yankees, in the mouth of men of color, is illogical, misplaced, and unfortunate." Besides, the outrage over Yankee adventurism was "more a symptom than the cause of this intense opposition." The real cause, according to Houzeau, was the Franco-Africans' "spirit of independence"; they simply could not accept the idea of English-speaking northerners dictating the future of their native state. Houzeau, on the other hand, emphasized that "one ought to be American before being Louisianian" and that it was "necessary to introduce this new [northern] element if one wants to break the Southern spirit." He also maintained that, morally, the *Tribune* was bound to support the nominating convention's candidates after having recognized the convention's legitimacy, and that, practically, Warmoth would only be a governor with restricted powers, not an absolute dictator. But, to Houzeau's dismay, the "Franco-African element preferred to have its own candidates, excluding all the Yankees, and consequently allying itself with men more or less tainted by Southernism." This decision, he warned Roudanez, would isolate the *Tribune*, raise a distracting "Louisiana question" instead of speeding along the crucial process of national reunification, and divide the Republican party so severely as to make a Democratic victory possible.[61]

Worst of all, Houzeau pointed out that the "politics of independent action" placed the "colored Franco-African element . . . in very sharp opposition to the colored element which speaks English," and threatened "to reopen the gap between the free born

61. Houzeau to his parents April 2, March 2, 1868, both in Houzeau Papers; Houzeau to N. C. Schmit, March 2, 1868, in Correspondance Houzeau-Schmit; Houzeau to Victor Bouvy, March 2, 1868, Houzeau to m. c. P. [mon cher (Charles) Potvin], March 2, 1868, both in Liagre Papers; Houzeau, "My Passage," 150. Houzeau later wrote that "the idea of repulsing the North and of 'gallicizing Louisiana' instead of Americanizing it was to march backwards in time." Houzeau to N. C. Schmit, May 9, 1868, in Correspondance Houzeau-Schmit.

mulattoes and the black freedmen (who are very partisan to the North). This division between the mulattoes and the blacks," he continued,

> I have worked three years to make disappear; I have succeeded in overcoming all the suspicions of the blacks (who after all have the numbers and thus control the elections). I have always maintained and shown that the two branches could have only one and the same politics, one and the same interest, before the common enemy—the proslavery forces. . . . But the old aristocratic spirit of the mulatto has reawakened, and today there are three parties: the proslavery people, the blacks (with the white radicals), and a little party of mulattoes (with some white malcontents). This last party is naturally destined, if you look at its numerical weakness and the illiberalism of its principles, to a certain failure.[62]

Houzeau pleaded with Roudanez to abandon "a road so dangerous," but to no avail. On January 18, 1868, he resigned from the *Tribune*, convinced that "my friends, too French in America, will be beaten in the elections, killing their influence forever."[63]

62. Houzeau, "My Passage," 150; Houzeau to N. C. Schmit, March 2, 1868, in Correspondance Houzeau-Schmit; Houzeau to his parents, April 2, 1868, in Houzeau Papers. Blassingame, *Black New Orleans*, 153, is troubled by Houzeau's description of black-mulatto relations within the Negro population of New Orleans: "Houzeau's criticism of the mulattoes was apparently based as much on the fact that they were not as revolutionary as he was as it was on their color prejudice." Although Blassingame speculates freely about Houzeau's motivation in emphasizing intraracial tensions, he apparently does so without having read either "My Passage" or Houzeau's substantial correspondence on the matter, for neither is cited anywhere in *Black New Orleans*. In both of these sources Houzeau suggests that the free coloreds' social prejudices and political convictions were part of a distinct world view that grew out of their particular color, class, and culture. For support of Houzeau's analysis, see Rankin, "Politics of Caste," 107–46; David C. Rankin, "The Impact of the Civil War on the Free Colored Community of New Orleans," *Perspectives in American History*, XI (1977–78), 377–416.

63. Houzeau to Victor Bouvy, March 2, 1868, in Liagre Papers. Although the

The Republican party and its supporters did everything in their power to make Houzeau's prediction come true. Less than two weeks after Roudanez bolted the convention, the central executive committee of the Republican party of Louisiana summarily expelled nine of its members who were loyal to Roudanez and replaced the *Tribune* with the pro-Warmoth *Republican* as the party's official journal. In February the party dispatched the white carpetbagger Thomas W. Conway to Washington, D.C., where he convinced the clerk of the U.S. House of Representatives to grant all future federal printing contracts to the pro-Warmoth St. Landry *Progress* instead of the *Tribune.* In early March Conway, the former head of the Freedmen's Bureau in Louisiana, publicly denounced Roudanez as a monarchist who preferred France to America and as a traitor who "would beat Warmoth if he had to join hands with the conservatives." Another outspoken critic was the Negro carpetbagger P. B. S. Pinchback, who called Roudanez "a man who would endanger the safety of his entire race, because he could not have everything just as he wanted it." He cautioned Louisiana Negroes "to be aware of how you listen to this hissing of the Serpent."[64]

---

owners remained steadfast in their opposition to Houzeau's position, they informed him that he could support the regular Republican ticket in the *Tribune.* But Houzeau, whose "convictions were so strong that nothing could change them," refused, explaining: "I declined to do so, not wanting to lay down the law to people whom I had come to help, and knowing furthermore that the position [adopted in the *Tribune*] would be false." Houzeau to N. C. Schmit, March 2, 1868, in Correspondance Houzeau-Schmit.

64. *Republican,* January 31, March 10, February 27, March 1, 4, 1868. Conway reported to Warmoth on his visit with Edward McPherson, clerk of the House of Representatives: "I told him [McPherson's aide] all about the *Tribune.* He knew it all and seemed just as mad as you are when you swear so. He took his hat and said, 'come, let us go up and see McPherson and get that printing away from Roudanez—he shant have it any longer.' We went. There in his corner chair, buried in newspapers, sat McPherson. I made short work of telling him about the *Tribune.* He too knew of it all and said—'Durant got that printing for that paper and I'm going to see him and tell him it's a darn swindle [as] the paper is now serving our enemies and I consider myself cheated and swindled.'" Conway to Warmoth, Feb-

The Republican press had a field day with Roudanez and the *Tribune*. The *Advocate* referred to Roudanez as "Napoleon" and accused the *Tribune* of making "insidious appeals to the old creole colored element." It condemned the men of the *Tribune* as a gang of "soreheaded bolters" whose attack upon Warmoth and other northern politicians "comes with bad grace from a paper edited by Frenchmen and Spaniards, who are not Americans in that

<hr>

ruary 15, 1868, in Henry Clay Warmoth Papers, Southern Historical Collection, University of North Carolina, Chapel Hill, N.C.

The Pinchback quotation is from a speech dated July 19, 1867, in the P. B. S. Pinchback Papers, Moreland-Spingarn Research Center, Howard University, Washington, D.C. For more on Pinchback's opposition to reconciliation with "that clique" at the *Tribune*, see *Republican*, July 2, 1867. Ironically, Pinchback's newspaper, the *Louisianian*, would later refer sorrowfully to the fact that quarreling among Negro leaders had resulted in the death of the *Tribune*, and Pinchback would declare in a speech that could have been written by Roudanez that Negro carpetbaggers "would sell Christ from the cross; they would go back on their party, on their friends and themselves." *Louisianian*, August 29, 1874, December 28, 1872.

Although Houzeau thought Pinchback correct in opposing Roudanez's bolting ticket, he apparently found little else noteworthy about him, for he fails even to mention the future lieutenant governor of Louisiana in "My Passage." The writings of Pinchback's grandson Jean Toomer suggest that Houzeau, the self-righteous reformer who called his work in New Orleans "a mission of philanthropy," would have found it difficult to say anything favorable about Pinchback. Toomer, the gifted Harlem Renaissance poet who was raised in his grandfather's home, doubted that Pinchback "saw himself bearing a mission to secure and maintain the rights of the freedmen." To Toomer, Pinchback was "an adventurer" who during his most altruistic moments employed "the tactics, not of an idealist and liberator, but of a bold dramatic venturer. More than anything else," Toomer believed, "Pinchback saw himself as a winner of a dangerous game. He liked to play the game. He liked to win. This—the reconstruction situation in Louisiana—was the chance his personal ambition had been waiting for. He was not a reformer. He was not primarily a fighter for a general human cause. He was, or was soon to become, a politician." The respected free colored leader Louis Martinet agreed with Toomer's assessment. In 1892 he singled out "Pinchback & the like" for special condemnation. "What," he asked, "have they ever done that has not been of more profit to them than to their race? *They have grown rich in fighting the race's battles*; that's the kind of patriots they are." Darwin T. Turner (ed.), *The Wayward and the Seeking: A Collection of Writings by Jean Toomer* (Washington, D.C., 1980), 24–25. Martinet is quoted in Rankin, "Origins of Negro Leadership," 162.

higher and nobler sense in which the majority of our 'New-comers' are." Appealing openly to the freedmen's "Americanism," the *Advocate* emphasized that "the very nomenclature of the *Tribune* is foreign, and its illustrations, even in its English editorials, are from French history and not American." The *Free South*, which was published by the Negro carpetbagger John W. Menard, judged the *Tribune* "guilty of base ingratitude and inconstancy" for joining the rebel press for "the unholy purpose of abusing, vilifying and persecuting Northern men," the very men who had "removed the chains of slavery."[65] The St. Landry *Progress*, with its biracial board of directors, attacked Taliaferro as a conservative who had been nominated solely by Roudanez, and warned that Taliaferro had been "an owner of men, women, and children, and the lessons and habits of youth and early manhood are likely to form the character and govern the conduct of old age." The *Republican* pictured Roudanez as a treacherous megalomaniac wielding "a great horse-whip" and declaring, "I'd rather see Beauregard or Jeff Davis governor of Louisiana than Warmoth."[66]

65. *Advocate*, n.d., quoted in the *Republican*, February 2, April 12, 19, 1868; *Free South*, n.d., quoted in the *Republican*, March 10, 1868. When Menard decided to add a French edition to the *Free South*, "he turned to me," Houzeau wrote, "for an editor, and I gave him one of my old employees." Houzeau to his parents, January 24, 1869, in Houzeau Papers.

66. St. Landry *Progress*, April 11, 1868, quoted in Mills, "James Govan Taliaferro," 77. Although most of the *Progress'* original stockholders were Negroes, the paper's founders also included a few whites. In the Frenchman C. E. Durand, the *Progress*, like the *Tribune*, had a radical white European editor. McTigue, "Forms of Racial Interaction," 176–78. The *Progress* could, of course, have applied its warning about the impact of prewar slaveholding upon postwar behavior to Dumas as well as Taliaferro. When another paper did attack Dumas, charging that it was "execrable for the colored man to have owned slaves under any conditions whatever," the *Tribune* retorted "that the serfs of Russia were as white as their masters." More tactfully, the paper maintained that Dumas had inherited his "many slaves," had kept them only because of antimanumission legislation, had treated them "as freemen," and had raised a company of Union soldiers from them during the Civil War. *Tribune*, July 2, 1867; *Republican*, April 5, March 28, 1868. Five years later Roudanez would, in fact, join the former Confederate General

On February 7, three weeks after Houzeau resigned, the *Republican* asked whether the *Tribune*, with its "imperial swag," had "gone . . . into other hands," for "all of its readers know that its editorials are written by a new hand, and dictated by a new spirit which has heretofore been unknown to its columns." A vivid example of this new spirit, according to the *Republican*, was the *Tribune*'s decision to publish and attribute to Oscar Dunn a virulently antimulatto speech. Dunn, in an open letter to the *Tribune*, declared that he had been "grossly misrepresented" and appealed to the editor to "hasten to undo the injury you have, I must believe, unintentionally done me as well as the Republican party." The *Tribune* responded by refusing even to print Dunn's letter and by continuing to publish the speech in an effort, the *Republican* charged, to get a copy of this "wholly *untrue*" speech "into every [colored] creole family in the state."[67] With the Republican press

---

P. G. T. Beauregard in an effort to rid Louisiana of northern white carpetbaggers and bring economic stability, honest government, and racial harmony to the state. See *Times*, May 28, 1873; T. Harry Williams, "The Louisiana Unification Movement of 1873," *Journal of Southern History*, XI (1945), 349–69.

67. *Republican*, February 7, March 27 (which reprints Dunn's March 23 letter to the editor of the *Tribune*), 22, 24, 25, 26, 1868. The *Tribune*'s version of Dunn's speech is unavailable for analysis, because virtually all issues of the paper for the months preceding the 1868 election have disappeared; but an editorial in the Shreveport *Southwestern* makes plausible the *Tribune*'s contention that its version was in fact a faithful reproduction of what Dunn had said. "The radicals," the editorial stated, "after using every effort to prevail on the quadroons of the State to vote for the [proposed] constitution without much success, have turned against them, and are now denouncing them for everything that is bad." One such radical, who had accompanied Dunn on his campaign trip through Plaquemines Parish, where he delivered his controversial speech on February 16, found it "extraordinary that the only danger to the ratification of this Louisiana constitution, which guarantees the fullest and most perfect liberty, and accords the most perfect equality . . . before the law, should come from colored men." He was also amazed that the "quadroon society, puffed up with the conceit of their heretofore anomalous condition, and fancying it really a condescension on their part to stoop to the colored race and own themselves a part of it, demanded as the price of this condescension all the offices, all the honors, and all the emoluments." Shreveport *Southwestern*, April 15, 1868, quoted in *Elections in Louisiana*, pt. 2, p. 127.

united in its opposition to Roudanez, the only sympathetic hearing the *Tribune* received was in the rebel press, which eagerly backed Taliaferro for governor and praised Roudanez for his "devotion to so noble a cause."[68]

In the election, which took place on April 17–18, the freedmen voted overwhelmingly for the Warmoth-Dunn ticket, and the Republicans won by a landslide.[69] Praising the Negro masses for having "given the most severe lesson to the little hateful spirits who only wanted to see them hobble," Houzeau wrote a Belgian friend that "the election vindicated my position in a stunning manner." The election also guaranteed the realization of another Houzeau prediction. On April 2 he had written that "among the blacks, the influence of the *Tribune* is naturally lost forever; and it is my personal opinion that the newspaper will cease to appear after the election." Barely a week after the votes were counted,

68. *Times*, March 4, 1868, quoted in *Republican*, March 10, 1868. See also *Crescent*, April 3, 1868, quoted in *Republican*, April 4, 1868; *Picayune*, n.d., quoted in *Elections in Lousiana*, pt. 2, pp. 123–24. The white press did not forget Roudanez's bold stand in the election of 1868. Twenty-two years later, at the time of Roudanez's death, the *Picayune* paid tribute to this "man of genius and cultivation" who in the *Tribune* had founded a newspaper "opposed to the 'carpet-bag' rule." *L'Abeille* also eulogized Roudanez as a "distinguished and cultivated spirit" who had founded a newspaper "supporting the principles of the Republican party, but above all battering a hideous and deadly species, known at the time as carpetbaggers." *Picayune*, March 12, 1890; *L'Abeille*, March 13, 1890.

69. Official returns show Warmoth beating Taliaferro 65,270 to 38,118 votes. Unofficial returns have Dunn beating Dumas 45,751 to 4,791 votes, with 22,204 votes going to Albert Voorhies, the unofficial candidate of the Democratic party. *Senate Reports*, 44th Cong., 2nd Sess., *Reports of the Committees of the Senate* (1876–77), IV, pt. 3, between pp. 2634–2635. Roudanez must have known that a crushing defeat was coming; according to Houzeau, the outlook was so bleak that his candidates withdrew from the election just as the balloting began. The *Tribune* had previously revealed misgivings about its strength among the freedmen. For instance, when the Warmoth group first challenged the *Tribune* forces for control of the Republican party by proposing the election of a new central executive committee, the *Tribune* balked, claiming that "hundreds and even thousands of new voters [*i.e.*, freedmen] are not yet enlightened as to the real value of men and things." Houzeau, "My Passage," 152; *Tribune*, April 30, 1867.

Roudanez shut down the *Tribune*. "We record with regret," the *Picayune* reported on April 27, "the fact that the New Orleans *Tribune*, the only newspaper both owned and edited by colored people at the South, and the only daily thus conducted in the whole Union, has been compelled to suspend publication for want of support." In contrast, Houzeau showed little sympathy for Roudanez, a man whom he had called "one of my best friends here" just six months before the election. "The colored press," he wrote his parents on May 9, "having sacrificed reputation and popularity to little hateful passions, is closed. Its politics have been repudiated by the immense mass—a crushing mass—of the colored population." He wrote on the same day to another Belgian that "the colored press is closed! What rapid justice! Only principles are a sure guide."[70]

If Houzeau felt vindicated by Warmoth's election, Roudanez no doubt felt vindicated by his administration. During his tenure as governor, Warmoth vetoed two civil rights bills, resisted integration of the public schools, refused to enforce the equal accommodations provision of the state constitution, and presided over one of the most corrupt administrations in the history of a notably corrupt state. In fact, Warmoth's excesses provoked Roudanez to revive the *Tribune* and to continue publishing it until sometime in 1871.[71]

After Roudanez revived the *Tribune*, he repeatedly asked Houzeau to return as editor. But Houzeau, who had sailed out of New Orleans on May 17, 1868, had no desire to return and "refused absolutely." In his thinking, he wrote from Jamaica in January, 1869, the position at the *Tribune* had from the outset been "only

70. Houzeau to N. C. Schmit, May 9, 1868, in Correspondance Houzeau-Schmit; *Picayune*, April 27, 1868; Houzeau to his parents, April 2, May 9, 1868, Houzeau to his father, October 23, 1867, all in Houzeau Papers.
71. On Warmoth's administration, see Taylor, *Louisiana Reconstructed*, 187–202.

temporary," and he was happy now to "come back to my liberty and to the work of my choice." That work centered primarily upon completing *Études sur les facultés mentales des animaux comparées à celles de l'homme*, but it also included producing an occasional article for the *Tribune* and writing a pamphlet entitled "Mon passage à la *Tribune* de la Nouvelle-Orléans."[72]

HOUZEAU composed and printed "My Passage" in September, 1870, on a press that he had brought to Jamaica from New Orleans. When it suddenly appeared a year and a half later in the *Revue de Belgique* under the title "Le journal noir, aux États-Unis, de 1863 à 1870," Houzeau wrote to his parents: "The 'Black Newspaper' is a title that they put on it in Brussels. The original is entitled 'My Passage at the New Orleans *Tribune*.' I did not expect to see it reprinted there, especially after this interval."[73]

72. Houzeau to his parents, January 24, 1869, in Houzeau Papers. I have been unable to find any of Houzeau's articles in the *Tribune* after he left for Jamaica, but see the article comparing free labor in Jamaica and Louisiana that is reprinted in the *National Anti-Slavery Standard* of October 30, 1869, and signed by the special correspondent of the New Orleans *Tribune*, "C[harles]. D[alloz]." Houzeau said of his correspondence for the *Tribune*: "I have addressed to the New Orleans *Tribune*, in order to appease it and make it accept my second refusal to return, a series of letters in English on the effects of the abolition of slavery in Jamaica. They are supposed to come from an American man of color, and they are signed D." Houzeau to his parents, December 17, 1869, in Houzeau Papers. Apparently, Roudanez did not easily relinquish his hope that someday Houzeau would return as editor of the *Tribune*. On December 5, 1870, two and a half years after sailing for Jamaica, Houzeau wrote to his brother Auguste that "the New Orleans *Tribune*, upon my fourth refusal to return, is suspended again, and this time probably for good." In Houzeau Papers. During the 1870s Houzeau sent articles from Jamaica to *Le Meschacébé*, another bilingual Louisiana newspaper with which he was friendly while editor of the *Tribune*. Published in St. John the Baptist Parish, *Le Meschacébé* was edited by Eugène Dumez, who, according to Tinker, "Bibliography of the French Newspapers," 273, 275, 347–48, had fled France in the wake of the Revolution of 1848. Houzeau to his parents, July 20, 1873, in Houzeau Papers; *Tribune*, June 19, 1867 (French ed.).

73. Houzeau to his brother Auguste, July 23, 1872, Houzeau to his parents, July 23, 1872, both in Houzeau Papers; Houzeau, "Le journal noir," 5–28,

Houzeau may not have been completely surprised upon discovering "My Passage" in the *Revue de Belgique*, for the *Revue* was edited by his old friends Charles Potvin and Eugene Van Bemel and was successor to the suppressed *Revue trimestrielle*, which had published his earlier articles on life in the Americas. Moreover, a close reading of "My Passage" leaves no doubt that Houzeau expected his audience to include European as well as American readers, an expectation that evidently prompted the comparative perspective that enriches his memoir. Nevertheless, according to the editors of the *Revue de Belgique*, the pamphlet was originally "written for America" and was "addressed by Houzeau to his [former] employers in order to give them an account of 'his passage at the *Tribune*.'" Unfortunately, there is no record of precisely how the men at the *Tribune* responded to Houzeau's memoir. All we know is that three months after it appeared, Roudanez again asked Houzeau to come back to New Orleans and resume his position as editor of the *Tribune*.[74]

Whatever Roudanez's opinion of "My Passage," historians will be delighted with Houzeau's memoir, for they have long recognized the *Tribune* as the most important Negro newspaper of the Civil War era. In 1910 even John R. Ficklen, who considered Reconstruction "a gigantic blunder" and Negroes "an inferior race," acknowledged that the *Tribune* was a "vigorously edited" and "very dangerous organ of opposition, which the conservatives rashly concluded to ignore" and which had "immense" influence in the nation's capital. In 1935 the great Afro-American histo-

---

97–122. Houzeau's choice of the word *passage* in the title of his memoir is intriguing, particularly since it was during his stay at the *Tribune* that Houzeau began "passing" for black and since "passing" had the same meaning then as it does now. See, for example, *Louisianian*, May 11, 1871; Charles Gayarré, "The Southern Question," *North American Review*, CXXV (1877), 492–93.

74. Houzeau, "Le journal noir," 5n–6n; Houzeau to his brother Auguste, December 5, 1870, in Houzeau Papers.

rian W. E. B. Du Bois also recognized the *Tribune* as "an unusually effective organ" and reproduced lengthy passages from it in his pioneering work on *Black Reconstruction in America*. More recently, Leon F. Litwack studded his prize-winning book on the aftermath of slavery with observations from the *Tribune*, which he singled out for its cogent and prophetic editorials as well as its "radical notions of reconstruction." And William S. McFeely has concluded in his important study of the Freedmen's Bureau that "it would be difficult to find a single publication of the Second Reconstruction as clear [as the *Tribune*] in stating Negro aims for complete equality in America or as optimistic about its accomplishment."[75]

Houzeau's memoir is a highly personal account of this extraordinary newspaper. In fact, it was too personal for the editors of the *Revue de Belgique*, who were embarrassed by Houzeau's decision to write in the first person and excused it as a bow to American literary taste. Otherwise, the editors were well-satisfied with Houzeau's style, for he generally tells his story in clear, straightforward prose that is often identical to the language found in the *Tribune* itself. At times he does abandon this fast-paced newspaper style and adopts a more leisurely and scholarly style that employs paradigms from the Great Chain of Being, Plenitude, and Civic Republicanism, but for the most part "My Passage" remains extremely accessible to the general reader. No one can read Houzeau's description of the New Orleans Riot, from which he was separated "by the thickness of a door," without being impressed

75. Ficklen, *History of Reconstruction*, 7, 179, 142, 143; Du Bois, *Black Reconstruction*, 456–72 (quotation on 456); Litwack, *Been in the Storm So Long*, 377, 512, 525, 526, 543 (quotation on 529); McFeely, *Yankee Stepfather*, 167–68. See also McPherson, *Negro's Civil War*, 346; and Joe Gray Taylor, "Civil War and Reconstruction," in Light T. Cummins and Glen Jeansonne (eds.), *A Guide to the History of Louisiana* (Westport, Conn., 1982), who writes on p. 45 that "unquestionably the most valuable single newspaper source [for the history of Reconstruction in Louisiana] is the New Orleans *Tribune*."

by his ability to convey the terror and excitement of Reconstruction in Louisiana.[76]

Overall, Houzeau's memoir is reliable as well as readable. There are a few factual errors—for example, Houzeau provides the wrong dates for the 1865 election of delegates to the Friends of Universal Suffrage Convention and for the adjournment of the 1868 Louisiana Constitutional Convention—but these are minor lapses of little consequence. Of greater concern is Houzeau's tendency to exaggerate the *Tribune*'s influence. Certainly, the *Tribune* had important friends in Washington, as Ficklen observed long ago, but it is misleading to imply, as Houzeau occasionally does, that the nation's political and military leaders were hanging on the paper's every word; indeed, the election of 1868 raises serious doubts about the *Tribune*'s strength even among Louisiana freedmen. Houzeau may also somewhat exaggerate his own influence at the *Tribune*. It is true that the paper's proprietors deemed his services invaluable, that after he left the paper never regained its previous quality, and that the claims Houzeau makes in "My Passage" about his contributions to the *Tribune* are strikingly consistent with the claims he made earlier in letters home. Nevertheless, one wishes that Roudanez, Trévigne, and others associated with the *Tribune* had left testimony about their part in the paper's production and management. As it is, Houzeau's memoir stands alone as the only insider's account of the nation's first black daily.

But "My Passage" is more than a history of the *Tribune*. It is also a brilliant survey of the struggle to bring economic opportunity, political democracy, and racial equality to postemancipation Louisiana. To this task Houzeau brought the radical racial and political ideas that give his memoir a remarkably modern ring and set his recollections apart from those of virtually all

76. Houzeau, "Le journal noir," 5n–6n; Houzeau to his parents, August 26, 1866, in Houzeau Papers.

other contemporary commentators on the postwar South. Perhaps it is Houzeau's "modern" perspective—a perspective which, for example, views suffrage as "the natural right of every woman" and advocates the election of Negroes to political office simply because they are Negroes—that explains why "My Passage" anticipates so many of the conclusions that historians have only recently reached.[77]

To Houzeau the postemancipation era was characterized, above all else, by a fierce battle between "an unjust and privileged ruling class" and "an oppressed class that had been trampled underfoot." As such, it was merely another episode in "the great universal fight of the oppressed of all colors and nations." But the fight in Louisiana, according to Houzeau, was unnecessarily violent and protracted because Andrew Johnson was a reactionary; because Congress lacked the courage to wage war on racial bigotry; because most northerners were indifferent to the fate of the freed-

---

77. *Tribune*, May 1, 1866; Houzeau, "My Passage," 148. Themes briefly touched upon in "My Passage" are more fully developed and documented in such diverse works as: Kenneth M. Stampp, *The Era of Reconstruction* (New York, 1965); C. Vann Woodward, *American Counterpoint: Slavery and Racism in the North-South Dialogue* (Boston, 1971), ch. 6; Litwack, *Been in the Storm So Long*; McFeely, *Yankee Stepfather*; Louis S. Gerteis, *From Contraband to Freedman: Federal Policy Toward Southern Blacks, 1861–1865* (Westport, Conn., 1973), esp. chs. 4–6; McCrary, *Abraham Lincoln*; Ripley, *Slaves and Freedmen*; Taylor, *Louisiana Reconstructed*; Vincent, *Black Legislators*.

In many respects the contemporary work closest to Houzeau's memoir is *A Fool's Errand*, Albion W. Tourgée's fictional account of his experiences in North Carolina during Reconstruction. Later Tourgée also worked with the Negro population of New Orleans in an effort to end racial segregation in Louisiana. Tourgée, *A Fool's Errand: A Novel of the South During Reconstruction* (New York, 1879); Woodward, *American Counterpoint*, ch. 8. The most famous Louisiana carpetbagger, Henry Clay Warmoth, left in *War, Politics and Reconstruction* a defensive, anti-Negro autobiography that bears no resemblance to Houzeau's memoir. Also very different is Rodolphe Lucien Desdunes' fascinating memoir, *Our People and Our History*. Only fifteen when the Civil War ended, Desdunes did not participate in Reconstruction politics, and unlike Houzeau, who sought to speak for the freed slaves, Desdunes was the proud spokesman of the hereditary free colored community.

men; because federal Reconstruction policy was timid, vacillating, and contradictory; because military commanders in the Department of the Gulf issued labor regulations that practically reestablished slavery; because the Freedmen's Bureau was understaffed and proplanter; because Yankee carpetbaggers were unprincipled opportunists; and especially because southern whites were incorrigible, intransigent, and racist.[78]

Houzeau's harsh judgment of southern whites and their "lying press" was not simply a function of his radical predilections. It was rather an opinion that he arrived at after living and working in Louisiana for three and a half years. In 1858 he had actually praised white Louisianians for their open-mindedness on the question of emancipation, and in 1864 he wrote that the time for fighting was over and that he would use his influence at the *Tribune* only "in a spirit of conciliation and humanity." As editor he would seek not only the "admission of men of color to public functions, that of their children to middle and high schools (we already have primary instruction), the alleviation of the lot of the freedmen, [and] the distribution of land to capable and hardworking Negroes," but also "the forgetting of past injuries, [and] the condemnation of vengeance for grievances alas too real. . . . If I can do good (not evil), however little it may be, I will do it." Six years later in "My Passage," Houzeau reiterated that the ideas he presented in the *Tribune* "would have led only to peace and conciliation as long as the rights acquired by the newly freed masses were respected."[79]

78. Houzeau, "My Passage," *passim* (quotations on 76, 75). Houzeau elaborates upon these themes in the *Tribune*. In "My Passage" he at least mentions most of them but says surprisingly little about two of his favorite targets, the Freedmen's Bureau and Andrew Johnson. See *Tribune*, August 31, December 14, 1865, February 15, September 11, 1866.

79. Houzeau to his parents, January 23, 1858, in Houzeau Papers; Houzeau to J.-B.-J. Liagre, November 2, 1864, in Liagre Papers; Houzeau, "My Passage," 92.

Houzeau believed his position to be both fair and farsighted. It was based upon justice—"and justice is the same for all men, whatever the shade of their skin"—and upon a conviction that during Reconstruction the United States, to achieve its potential greatness, would have to undergo racial as well as regional reconciliation. Thus he writes in his memoir: "Give us equality before the law, equality in schooling, equality in public hiring, and you will have one indivisible people; and by the year 1900 . . . you will have formed the most powerful agglomeration that civilization has ever known, you will constitute a unified and great nation."[80]

But Houzeau's efforts at persuasion failed before the "immense power" of racism, and white defiance intensified until it finally exploded in the bloody riot of 1866. The riot shattered Houzeau's hope for voluntary reconciliation; it even seemed to shake his faith in the humanity of southern whites. The day after the riot he cried: "*Ces esclavagistes sont des démons.*" He now called for the "iron hand" of the state to eradicate racial prejudice and the oppression that inevitably accompanies it. Prejudice, Houzeau writes in "My Passage," has "to be overthrown by force. Prejudice is not a matter of reason; it is absurd, then, to expect it to yield to rational argument." In sum, he believed southern whites were "blind men whose passions endangered their most cherished interests." Primary responsibility for the long and antagonistic nature of Reconstruction rested squarely on their shoulders.[81]

Houzeau also suggests in "My Passage" that divisions within the Negro community itself hampered the struggle for equality. To be sure, his account is highly laudatory toward the men of the *Tribune* and contains none of the bitterness found in his final

80. Houzeau, "My Passage," 82, 96.
81. Houzeau to N. C. Schmit, July 31, 1866, in Correspondance Houzeau-Schmit; Houzeau, "My Passage," 103, 119, 117, 123.

letters from New Orleans; but it is not a superficial paean to Louisianians of African descent. Houzeau writes with refreshing candor of the formidable differences of color, class, and culture that separated the old freeborn men of color and the newly emancipated freedmen, a separation that resulted in many free coloreds distinguishing "their struggle from that of the Negroes" and believing that "they would achieve their cause more quickly if they abandoned the black to his fate." Houzeau frankly admits that he experienced "great difficulty" in trying to unite the free and the freed in a single phalanx. Thus, although he was totally committed to the Negro cause—he wrote in 1866 that "there is nothing I would not do for these poor people"—Houzeau was not an uncritical ally. As a "scientific socialist," he held a position similar to that of Du Bois, who, a half century later, wrote that the purpose of writing the history of Reconstruction was not, among other things, "to prove that Negroes were black angels," but "simply to establish the Truth, on which Right in the future may be built."[82]

But if Houzeau found much to criticize about Reconstruction, he found even more to celebrate. In retrospect, all the delays and disappointments faded to insignificance before the overwhelming fact that the emancipation and rehabilitation of four million slaves constituted a social revolution of staggering proportions. Summing up his view of Reconstruction in "My Passage," Houzeau writes: "Our hearts rejoiced at the tardy and yet so nobly conceived and thoroughly executed reparation of long-standing injustice and nameless oppression. If we had cast stones at the United States because it had tolerated slavery, how we could praise it for the way in which it set things right!" In an age that experienced a wide variety of emancipations and reconstructions

82. Houzeau, "My Passage," 81, 82; Houzeau to his mother, November 18, 1866, in Houzeau Papers; Du Bois, *Black Reconstruction*, 725.

throughout the world, the American experiment stood alone. It was, according to Houzeau, "without doubt the greatest event of our times."[83]

For Houzeau, the centerpiece of this "social transformation" was the abolition of slavery. Emancipation destroyed forever a way of life that was based upon the ownership of men and women. No longer would Negro workers be bought and sold like cattle; no longer would they be compelled to labor from sunup to sundown simply because of the accident of birth. Congressional legislation also guaranteed that they would no longer be denied basic civil and political rights solely on the basis of their race. Houzeau found it impossible to overemphasize the importance of Negro suffrage. To him "it was obvious that in a government where the major offices are elective, any class denied the vote is necessarily sacrificed: it obtains neither equal justice, nor the redress of wrongs, nor even its rightful part of protection in society." Houzeau further believed, though he is silent on this point in "My Passage," that the franchise was an instrument with which labor could battle capital, with which one could destroy a "class government" that had previously been controlled by men of wealth and property. If one needed proof that the right to vote was "the culmination, the crowning achievement," of Reconstruction, one had only to look at Louisiana in 1868: half the delegates to the state constitutional convention were Negroes, a third of the state house of representatives were Negroes, the state treasurer was a Negro, and so was the lieutenant governor. Similar conditions obtained in other

83. Houzeau, "My Passage," 144–45. On the aftermath of other efforts to emancipate involuntary labor, see George M. Fredrickson, "After Emancipation: A Comparative Study of White Responses to the New Order of Race Relations in the American South, Jamaica & the Cape Colony of South Africa," in David G. Sansing (ed.), *What Was Freedom's Price?* (Jackson, Miss., 1978), 71–92; C. Vann Woodward, "The Price of Freedom," in *ibid.*, 93–113; Jerome Blum, *The End of the Old Order in Rural Europe* (Princeton, 1978).

southern states, but in no other society in the Western Hemisphere during the nineteenth century, except postrevolutionary Haiti, did former slaves acquire such genuine political power.[84]

Houzeau was also impressed by the freedmen's economic progress. He says surprisingly little in "My Passage" about the need to distribute land among the freedmen, an objective that he had consistently supported in his editorials at the *Tribune* and in his work for the New Orleans Freedmen's Aid Association and the Louisiana Homestead Association. Instead, he stresses that sharecropping, however exploitative, should not be confused with slavery; and he predicts that small, hardworking Negro farmers would one day be the backbone of garden agriculture in the South. Houzeau's emphasis on the ability of the independent Negro farmer to make it on his own should not be interpreted as an endorsement of competitive commerce. It should be understood, rather, as an affirmation of his belief in the Negro race, for one of the major goals of "My Passage" is to demonstrate that Afro-Americans are the equal of white Americans and thus welcome a truly free society in which "each person is the product of his own deeds." Like other early socialist intellectuals, Houzeau was inspired by a profound reverence for the sanctity of the individual. The collective dimension of his thought was simply an insistence that all men must have the right to become complete human beings.[85]

Houzeau's faith in the future, belief in racial equality, and commitment to integral democracy set him apart from most American intellectuals of the postwar era. Disillusioned by the war and its aftermath, the latter were often social pessimists who succumbed

84. Houzeau, "My Passage," 148, 121, 111; *Tribune*, October 22, 1867; Vincent, *Black Legislators*, 47, 71; Woodward, "The Price of Freedom," 109.

85. Houzeau, "My Passage," 147, 94. For a lucid discussion of early socialist thought, see Martin Malia, *Alexander Herzen and the Birth of Russian Socialism* (Cambridge, Mass., 1961), chs. 6, 10, 13.

all too readily to an emerging pseudo-scientific racism and advocated a new elitism to replace the democratic dogmas of the past. They sought new laws to discipline society, and their approach to reform was conservative, tough-minded, and practical. Houzeau, on the other hand, remained an irrepressible optimist and idealistic visionary who believed in the inevitable march of progress. He retained the "come-outer" spirit that had characterized the most radical reformers of antebellum America, and his memoir serves not only as an account of his passage at the New Orleans *Tribune*, but also as a challenge to those who hide behind the walls of the academy to follow in his footsteps and "come-out."[86]

86. On the decline of the humanitarian impulse among American intellectuals, see George M. Fredrickson, *The Inner Civil War: Northern Intellectuals and the Crisis of the Union* (New York, 1965).

My Passage at the New Orleans *Tribune*

Jean-Charles Houzeau

N February, 1863, I arrived in New Orleans after having left—not without difficulty— Confederate territory, then in the throes of violent despotism. I went under the pseudonym of Dalloz, under which I had escaped.[1] It was useless for me to look back. Texas was closed to me forever, even if the North won the war and peace were restored; the party vengeance in these semidesert, semisavage regions is both too implacable and too easily executed with impunity. I was now in a city under Federal authority, and here I was comparatively safe.

Nevertheless, the capital of Louisiana, although conquered, was not beaten. The Confederacy was too close and was maintaining itself with such power that illusions and hopes continued to run high. The "Caucasian" population of New Orleans was, almost without exception, in favor of the proslavery forces, and the city had a large number of very fanatical secret societies.[2] This

1. When Houzeau arrived in New Orleans on January 31, 1863, he used the pseudonym Charles J. Dalloz, which might be a corruption of the pronunciation of his own surname with the order of his first two initials reversed, a reference to the respected French publishing house of the time, or a tribute to the famous Dalloz family, the members of which were progressive lawyers, journalists, and politicians in nineteenth-century France. On the Dalloz family, see J. Balteau *et al.* (eds.), *Dictionnaire de biographie française* (Paris, 1933–), X, 1–4.

2. A significant number of white New Orleanians had opposed secession, and

large city has always remained more hostile than any other to the Federal government and to the northern states. Even today, it is more of an enemy than Charleston or Montgomery. Indeed, it only experienced the good days of the Confederacy, for by the end of the first year of the war, it had fallen under Union control.[3] The other cities of the South, on the other hand, had gone through the period of terror, mass conscription, famine, retreat, and shellings. They witnessed sufferings that left them with only one desire—to see the war end—whereas the people of New Orleans, who were spared all of these sufferings, were for this same reason more stubborn and more warlike.

Thus, while the Federal authorities were in power, the white population chafed at the bit with haughty impatience. Their self-important press provided them with false news and helped to maintain foolish hopes. A small paper, the *Era*, edited by a Federal officer, provided the only counterweight to the immense influence of the proslavery forces; but it had hardly one reader for every five hundred inhabitants. It was soon forced to cease publication despite the patronage of the government.[4] It was replaced by a short-lived paper, then nothing more was heard, at least for a time, in favor of the Union and liberty in the great metropolis of the Mississippi.

---

shortly after the Union invasion a small body of them began working to restore Louisiana to the Union. See Gerald M. Capers, *Occupied City: New Orleans Under the Federals, 1862–1865* (Lexington, Ky., 1965), 20–24; Peyton McCrary, *Abraham Lincoln and Reconstruction: The Louisiana Experiment* (Princeton, 1978).

3. New Orleans fell to Union naval forces on April 25, 1862; the bombardment of Fort Sumter began on April 12, 1861. On the fall of New Orleans, see John D. Winters, *The Civil War in Louisiana* (Baton Rouge, 1963), ch. 12.

4. The *Era*, which replaced the pro-Union *Daily Delta* on February 15, 1863, was edited by two northerners, A. C. Hill and A. G. Hill. Prior to its collapse in January, 1865, the *Era* reportedly had a readership of nearly twenty thousand. Capers, *Occupied City*, 178–81; Fayette Copeland, "The New Orleans Press and the Reconstruction," *Louisiana Historical Quarterly*, XXX (1947), 301–303. (The *Era* and all other newspapers cited hereinafter are from New Orleans unless otherwise noted.)

Men of color, it is true, had been printing for the last few months a small newspaper, at first a weekly and which now appeared thrice-weekly, called *L'Union*,[5] and its chief editor, Paul Trévigne,[6] a man of color himself, defended with remarkable talent the principles that would lead to the freeing of his race. At that time it was very bold for the proscribed class to publish a newspaper and with a tone of wounded dignity to demand the return of its natural rights. The planters, faithful to their traditions, spoke openly of ransacking the printing plant and destroying the house where it was located. Nor would it have been difficult to make this threat come true. The military authorities at this time had little interest in the free men of color of New Orleans, whom they almost confused with slaves.[7] *L'Union* was published in French,[8]

5. *L'Union* was a biweekly from its first day of publication on September 27 until December 20, 1862; thereafter, beginning on December 23, 1862, it was a triweekly. The paper announced that it was suspending publication on May 31, 1864, but struggled on until finally disbanding on July 19, 1864.

6. Paul Trévigne (1825–1908), a free man of color, was born and reared in New Orleans. A man of modest means who in 1861 owned property valued at $500, he was prior to the Civil War a language teacher at the Institution Catholique des Orphelins Indigents. Trévigne also worked for the *Tribune* and two other Negro newspapers, the *Louisianian* and *Le Crusader*. Houzeau described Trévigne as a "gay spirit with literary tastes" who had "descended from a Spanish father" and had "a little of the pride (the good kind) of a Castilian character." New Orleans, Treasurer's Office, Tax Register, 1861–1862, p. 81, in City Hall Archives, New Orleans Public Library, New Orleans, La.; David C. Rankin, "The Origins of Negro Leadership in New Orleans During Reconstruction," in Howard N. Rabinowitz (ed.), *Southern Black Leaders of the Reconstruction Era* (Urbana, 1982), 188; Rodolphe Lucien Desdunes, *Our People and Our History: A Tribute to the Creole People of Color in Memory of the Great Men They Have Given Us and of the Good Works They Have Accomplished*, trans. and ed. Sister Dorothea Olga McCants (1911; Baton Rouge, 1973), 66–68; Houzeau to his parents, July 23, 1865, in Jean-Charles Houzeau Papers, Centre National d'Histoire des Sciences, Bibliothèque Royale Albert 1er, Brussels, Belgium (cited hereinafter as Houzeau Papers).

7. The free colored press repeatedly reminded federal officers that there had been a very large free colored as well as slave population in antebellum New Orleans. See, for example, *L'Union*, October 1, 1862, August 20, 1863; *Tribune*, August 4 (French ed.), December 29, 1864.

8. *L'Union* was published in both English and French beginning in early July, 1863.

which the Federal officers did not understand. Its editors were in no-man's-land, and their opponents could dare to do anything against them. But Trévigne, surrounded by a few brave friends, was prepared to defend himself and, since the men of color were Unionists, to fall draped in the American flag.[9]

This attack, however, at first put off from day to day, never came off as planned. Even so, the scornful hostility of the conspirators had not lost any of its violence when, upon my arrival in New Orleans, I visited the intrepid editors. I soon threw in my lot with them. *L'Union*, which when it passed a little later under the control of the Roudanez brothers[10] became a daily and was renamed the *Tribune*,[11] formed the center around which the boldest colored men of New Orleans rallied.

Before the suppression of slavery, there were twenty thousand persons of African descent in Louisiana who were free.[12] For most of them this status had been inherited from three or four gen-

9. Trévigne was no stranger to violence. His father had fought with Andrew Jackson at the Battle of New Orleans in 1815, and he himself had fought a duel in 1854. Desdunes, *Our People and Our History*, 66; *Picayune*, January 17, 1854.

10. Louis Charles and Jean Baptiste Roudanez are discussed above, 25–29.

11. In July, 1864, Louis Charles Roudanez and his associates bought the defunct *L'Union* and renamed it the *Tribune*. A bilingual triweekly at the time of its first issue on July 21, 1864, the *Tribune* was published daily, except Monday, from October 4, 1864, until it suspended publication on April 25, 1868. The *Tribune* was later revived and continued to be published irregularly until sometime in 1871. Few issues are extant for 1868 or after; the last surviving issue, which is in the newspaper collection of the American Antiquarian Society, Worcester, Mass., is apparently that of March 5, 1870. Houzeau to J.-B.-J. Liagre, November 2, 1864, in J.-B.-J. Liagre Papers, Archives, Académie Royale des Sciences, des Lettres et des Beaux-Arts de Belgique, Brussels, Belgium (cited hereinafter as Liagre Papers); Houzeau to N. C. Schmit, May 9, 1868, in Correspondance J.-C. Houzeau-N. C. Schmit, Archives, Université Libre de Bruxelles, Brussels, Belgium (cited hereinafter as Correspondance Houzeau-Schmit); *Daily Crusader*, March 22, 1890, quoted in Charles B. Rousseve, *The Negro in Louisiana: Aspects of His History and His Literature* (New Orleans, 1937), 115, 119; Copeland, "New Orleans Press," 321.

12. The free colored population of Louisiana in 1860 was 18,647. Bureau of the Census, *Population of the United States in 1860 . . .* (Washington, D.C., 1864), 191.

erations. The French settlers had been more generous than the American. Many of these free persons of color lived in financial ease. Even though almost all liberal professions and public offices were closed to them, they were able to engage in commerce and agriculture. A few had acquired fortunes. Hence, since schools at all levels were without exception closed to colored children, who were never to find themselves on an equal footing with white children, the rich and well-to-do families sent the young people of African blood to the schools of Paris and London, where many distinguished themselves.[13] These educated men, whose intelligence had been developed not only by study but by travel and knowledge of foreign countries as well, shuddered at the thought of themselves being rejected and scorned. Having been exposed to the liberal institutions of France and England, and having enjoyed civil equality, they chafed under the galling and iniquitous yoke of the Code Noir.[14] Among them was Joseph Tinchant, who soon thereafter left for Mexico and who spoke with the fire of a tribune.[15] Another was Dr. Roudanez, who had studied medicine in Paris and who steadfastly demanded and claimed his rights to

13. On the extraordinary achievements of the Louisiana free colored population, see Donald E. Everett, "Free Persons of Color in New Orleans, 1803–1865" (Ph.D. dissertation, Tulane University, 1952); H. E. Sterkx, *The Free Negro in Ante-Bellum Louisiana* (Rutherford, N.J., 1972); David C. Rankin, "The Forgotten People: Free People of Color in New Orleans, 1850–1870" (Ph.D. dissertation, Johns Hopkins University, 1976); Gary B. Mills, *The Forgotten People: Cane River's Creoles of Color* (Baton Rouge, 1977).

14. The Louisiana Code Noir, promulgated by the French in 1724 but often amended prior to the Civil War, enumerated the rights and obligations of free and enslaved persons of African descent. For a brief discussion of the Code and its impact, see David C. Rankin, "The Tannenbaum Thesis Reconsidered: Slavery and Race Relations in Antebellum Louisiana," *Southern Studies*, XVIII (1979), 5–31.

15. A free colored native of Louisiana, Joseph Tinchant was a successful merchant with a store on St. Charles Avenue. After serving in the Union Army, he became disgusted with the treatment accorded Negroes by federal officials and on August 24, 1864, removed his family to Mexico. *Tribune*, August 25, 1864 (French ed.).

their fullest extent with a strength of soul that I always admired. And there was Dumas, who was currently a major in Butler's regiment.[16] There was also Delassize, a man well known in Belgium;[17] in the background were Soulié,[18] Joubert,[19] and Clay,[20] who were

16. Francis Ernest Dumas (1837–1901) was a free man of color who served as a major in the Louisiana Native Guards that were raised in 1862 under the auspices of Union General Benjamin F. Butler. A native of New Hampshire, Butler (1818–1893) was commanding general of the Department of the Gulf from May–December, 1862. He later served as a Republican congressman from Massachusetts from 1867–1875. In 1863 Butler testified about Dumas before the American Freedmen's Inquiry Commission: "I think he is some distant relation of Alexander Dumas. He is a man who would be worth a quarter of a million, in reasonably good times. . . . He had more capability as Major, than I had as Major-General, I am quite sure, if knowledge of affairs, and every thing that goes to make up a man, is any test." Ezra J. Warner, *Generals in Blue: Lives of the Union Commanders* (Baton Rouge, 1964), 60–61; Ira Berlin *et al.* (eds.), *Freedom: A Documentary History of Emancipation, 1861–1867*, Series II: *The Black Military Experience* (Cambridge, 1982), 313–14. Dumas is also discussed above, 48.

17. Louis Théodule Delassize, a light-colored mulatto who on the eve of the Civil War owned two slaves worth $1300, was born in Louisiana in 1818. Inventor of the Delassize American Needlegun, he owned property valued at $20,500 in 1870. During Reconstruction he served as city recorder of conveyances and administrator of public works. New Orleans, Treasurer's Office, Tax Ledger, 1861, A–E, p. 337; Manuscript Census Returns, Ninth Census, 1870, Louisiana, X, 139, Records of the U.S. Bureau of the Census, in Record Group 29, National Archives; *House Miscellaneous Documents*, 42nd Cong., 2nd Sess., No. 211, *Testimony Taken by the Select Committee to Investigate the Condition of Affairs in the State of Louisiana* (1872), (cited hereinafter as *Condition of Affairs in Louisiana*), 453; *Republican*, May 13, 1871. See also the interesting poem addressed to Delassize in the *Tribune*, December 30, 1866 (French ed.).

18. Bernard A. Soulié, a free man of color, was born in New Orleans in 1803. A commission merchant who in 1861 owned property, including three slaves, valued at $100,150, Soulié usually remained in the background and occasionally declined political office because of pressing business commitments. Rankin, "Origins of Negro Leadership," 167, 188.

19. Blanc F. Joubert, a free man of color who could easily pass for white, was born in New Orleans in 1816, the son of a Frenchman from whom he inherited two slaves. In 1872 he owned property valued at over $40,000. Joubert lived in Paris from 1859 to 1864; after returning to New Orleans, he served as United States assessor of internal revenue and as a commissioner of the New Orleans metropolitan police. *Condition of Affairs in Louisiana*, 453–62; *Republican*, March 7, 1874; Rankin, "Origins of Negro Leadership," 164, 185.

20. John Racquet Clay, a very light-colored free Negro, was born in New Or-

important in commerce and were more circumspect in their participation in the movement even though no less devoted to it. The English-speaking free element was represented by Dunn,[21] whose skin was black as ebony and who was later elected lieutenant governor of Louisiana by his racial brothers. By limiting myself to these names, I do not wish to lessen the merit of others. There were simply too many men in the inner circle for me to do justice to every one. Hearts were so well disposed, intentions so solidly fixed, and nearly everywhere such generous devotion to the cause, that it would be unjust to separate a few of them from the group that surrounded and fortified them.

I liked to spend time with these pariahs of the proslavery society. At the time when the most rigid prejudice forbade the white man from having any social contact with the black man or the colored man, I took delight in openly shaking hands with these outcasts: this was my protest. The cause that the "Negro newspaper" was defending was after all only one chapter in the great universal fight of the oppressed of all colors and nations. Whether the victim is called serf in Russia, peasant in Austria, Jew in Prussia, proletarian in France, pariah in India, Negro in the United States, at heart it is the same denial of justice. I understood the situation of colored men in New Orleans; I easily identified myself with them,

---

leans in 1829. A slaveholder prior to the war, Clay was an exchange broker who in 1870 held $20,000 in real estate. During Reconstruction he declined several political offices, but in 1871 he agreed to serve on the city school board. Clay committed suicide on March 8, 1879. *Condition of Affairs in Louisiana*, 453; David C. Rankin, "The Impact of the Civil War on the Free Colored Community of New Orleans," *Perspectives in American History*, XI (1977–78), 397, 405; Rankin, "Origins of Negro Leadership," 167, 183.

21. Oscar James Dunn, who during Reconstruction was an investigating agent for the Freedmen's Bureau, secretary of the advisory committee of the Freedmen's Saving and Trust Company, and from 1868 until his sudden death on November 22, 1871, lieutenant governor of Louisiana, is discussed above, 47, and in Marcus B. Christian, "The Theory of the Poisoning of Oscar J. Dunn," *Phylon*, VI (1945), 254–66.

for even though the individuals were different, the cause was nothing new or strange to me: on one hand I found an unjust and privileged ruling class, and on the other an oppressed class that had been trampled underfoot and had no role in society. From that moment on I contributed to the publication of the "Negro newspaper," and when a few months later I left for the North, I continued to submit articles regularly.[22]

I had been writing for a while from Philadelphia when I received an offer from Dr. Roudanez to edit the newspaper. It was now October, 1864. The struggle on the battlefields dragged on indecisively. The abolition of slavery, decreed in principle, was far from being a reality.[23] Not only were the eight states where the Confederacy held exclusive power obstinately opposed to emancipation,[24] but also the majority of northerners treated fugitive blacks with a harshness that hinted that slavery would survive under another name.[25] The letters that I received from Europe were in no way encouraging. Several of my friends, maintaining a pru-

22. Houzeau left New Orleans in early July, 1863, on the steamer *George Washington* and arrived in Philadelphia on July 23. There, under the pseudonym Cham, he served as northern correspondent for *L'Union* and subsequently for the *Tribune*. Houzeau to his parents, July 24, 1863, Houzeau to J.-B.-J. Liagre, November 2, 1864 (copy), both in Houzeau Papers. For examples of Houzeau's analysis of northern political and military affairs, see *L'Union*, September 22, 1863, January 5, 12, 16, 21, 28, April 19, May 19, 24, June 23, July 9, 1864; *Tribune*, July 26 (French ed.), August 11 (French ed.), September 1 (French ed.), November 15 (French ed.), 1864.

23. Houzeau is reminding the reader that the Emancipation Proclamation at the time of its announcement had not actually freed any slaves and that nearly two years after its implementation on January 1, 1863, the vast majority of southern slaves remained in bondage. See John H. Franklin, *The Emancipation Proclamation* (Edinburgh, 1963).

24. Houzeau is referring to Virginia, North Carolina, South Carolina, Georgia, Florida, Alabama, Mississippi, and Texas.

25. On northern racism in the Civil War era, see V. Jacque Voegeli, *Free But Not Equal: The Midwest and the Negro During the Civil War* (Chicago, 1967); George M. Fredrickson, *The Black Image in the White Mind: The Debate on Afro-American Character and Destiny, 1817–1914* (New York, 1971), chs. 4–6.

dent reserve, refrained from speaking to me about American affairs; only one of them, P.,[26] let his ardor shine through and maintained his faith in liberty and progress. But many others did not hesitate to assert that neither the emancipation of blacks nor the maintenance of government of the people, by the people, had any chance of success in the "disunited states." I was told that the prejudice based on skin color was an invincible prejudice. It was folly to believe that the Americans could change in this regard. My own belief that abolition would succeed was seen as the result of an error in judgment. My friends wrote me that, were I in Europe, I would see things in a wider and clearer perspective; I would then know that the break-up of the United States was an inevitable fact against which all resistance was absurd, and that the abolition of slavery would succeed only if it were brought about by the planters.

I was not unaware that Europe had been fooled and that many of its intelligent men claimed to know what they did not really know. This was later proved by events in both the United States and Mexico.[27] But these events had not yet occurred. The issues of

26. Houzeau is probably referring to the liberal Belgian writer Charles Potvin (1818–1902). See Gustave Vanwelkenhuyzen, "Charles Potvin," in the Belgian *Biographie nationale*, XXXIV, supplément 6 (1968), 664–70. Potvin had written in the *Revue trimestrielle* in 1857: "Mr. Houzeau possesses a profound scientific knowledge, a sweeping vision, a masterful analysis, a grand synthesis, a creative genius: in him science has a new Humboldt, a Belgian Humboldt." Quoted in Albert B. M. Lancaster, "J.-C. Houzeau: Notes biographiques," in J.-C. Houzeau and A. Lancaster, *Bibliographie générale de l'astronomie* (2 vols.; Brussels, 1889), I, pt. 2, p. xix.

27. Houzeau is referring to the defeat of the Confederacy in the United States in 1865 and the defeat and execution of Maximilian in Mexico in 1867. Houzeau was appalled at Europeans' misconceptions about slavery and the South. In 1863 he wrote a Belgian friend: "In your comfortable sitting rooms there yonder, you don't know the amount of misery that the slaveowners impose on the loyal inhabitants of the South." Houzeau to N. C. Schmit, June 24, 1863, in Correspondance Houzeau-Schmit. See also Houzeau to his mother, November 22, 1864, in Houzeau Papers. In *Question de l'esclavage* (Brussels, 1863), esp. chs. 2–3, 7, Houzeau tried to impress upon European readers the violence and "gross barbarism" (p. 64) that characterized the South because of slavery.

this great conflict had been poorly delineated. Russell, the London *Times* correspondent who was accompanying the Confederate army, called his letters materials "on the history of the decadence and fall of the American Republic."[28] The future presented itself, therefore, in somber colors.

In this time of doubt, the converging of so many discouraging opinions could only shake conviction and paralyze action. Would I then, I asked myself, go into battle deluded, like a man without judgment, for a cause that was practically impossible? Would I expose myself to loss of caste and to becoming a social pariah in order to defend a cause that is declared in advance to be lost, where all efforts are in vain, and where the battle will soon be a useless sacrifice and consequently a criminal one? Am I entering the leadership of the abolitionists, so to speak, after defeat, to participate in the last hours of a terrible debacle that will sweep me along in its wake? I put these letters back in their envelopes, returned them to the case from which I had taken them, and wrote my letter of acceptance. On November 14, 1864, I took up the editorship of the *Tribune*.

I returned to the group whose members were already known to me and whom I sought to describe above. Here was a core of men of African race, who in their intelligence, sense of rectitude, commercial talents, and acquired wealth, held a peculiar place, a unique place, in the southern states. Here was a sort of elite; here was the vanguard of the African population of the United States. It was evident that, on the day on which abolition became a fact, when the country would have to deal with the consequences of this great reform, this nucleus of Louisiana colored men would be

28. *In his account of the Battle of Fredricksburg, December 13, 1862.*—HOUZEAU. (This and all subsequent notes provided by Houzeau are in italics and are followed by his name.) William Howard Russell, the famous English correspondent, had published his observations on the first months of the American Civil War in *My Diary North and South* (2 vols.; London, 1863).

called upon to form the highest group of representatives, a sort of tutor to the black population of the Republic. In its favor, in effect, were education, knowledge, fortune, and experience in the practice of liberty. At a time when thousands of freedmen would be thrown onto the street, so to speak, where and when they would have to come to grips with their new situation and make their way in the world, would they not look to their elders in their search for guides, to those of their race who had preceded them? And on the other hand, to whom would the liberal party,[29] the Congress, and the government turn in order to learn the needs, the ideas, and the dangers of the population of African descent in the new order of things if not to these natural representatives, to these enlightened spokesmen for the black and colored population?

Since the *Tribune* was the newspaper of this elite corps, it became necessary to broaden its mission, to prepare for the future, by immediately making it the organ of five million black and brown-skinned men of the United States.[30] I undertook, therefore, to transform a local newspaper into a newspaper of national importance. Rather than speaking in the name and interest of a small group, the *Tribune*, I thought, should defend the masses of the proscribed race and unite this oppressed population completely around its standard. I was fortunate enough to achieve this idea of unity, which in turn reinforced our position. But in 1864 there were two obstacles which, had they not been removed, would have opposed the realization of this project.

The first was that the *Tribune* had been founded as a French-language newspaper.[31] This was the preferred language, very

29. The Republican party.

30. In 1870 there were 4,880,009 Afro-Americans in the United States, of whom 4,295,960 were black and 584,049 were mulatto. Bureau of the Census, *Negro Population, 1790–1915* (Washington, D.C., 1918), 208.

31. The *Tribune* was bilingual from the publication of its first issue on July 21, 1864.

often the only language, of the colored families that composed the elite corps. Isolated from society and its changes, these families had preserved the old language of the region, the language of their benefactors. Here was a touching homage to the memory of the liberality of the French Creoles.[32] But this proved a mistake because the use of this language, now a foreign one in the land, kept these colored men apart from the general life of the country. Slaveowners in fact had been very careful to favor this tendency, for on the day when these men of mixed blood might decide to speak out, they would be understood only by their own small group; they could not speak to the government of their country, the Congress, the northern press, public opinion, or their fellow citizens—nor could they make themselves understood by even the five million black slaves.[33] This obstacle had always seemed to me to be the biggest one of all. Nor was I the only one to point it out. Since the beginning of 1864, the *Tribune* had appeared in both languages. For a long time, however, the English section was only a cut-and-paste collection from English newspapers. On the contrary, it needed to become a veritable "tribune," from which one spoke to the government and to the country. Because of this necessity, I overcame my repugnance to writing in a language that I had learned only late in life.[34] Hereafter, the sole object of the

32. Houzeau is using the term *Creole* to describe someone of European descent born in the New World. Houzeau maintained that the French Creoles were both unusually tolerant in their dealings with free coloreds and brutally repressive in their treatment of slaves. Houzeau to his parents, July 22, 1866, in Houzeau Papers. For a discussion of this theme, see Rankin, "Tannenbaum Thesis," 5–31.

33. There were 3,953,760 slaves and 488,070 free Negroes in the United States in 1860. Bureau of the Census, *Population of the United States in 1860*, 598–99.

34. Houzeau had studied English intensely in 1857 in both London and New Orleans; during the 1860s he even wrote a few of his letters home in English. He nevertheless remained unsure of himself in English and had an employee at the *Tribune* carefully review all his English-language copy before sending it to press. Lancaster, "J.-C. Houzeau," xxviii, xxxii; Houzeau to N. C. Schmit, June 24, 1863, May 28, December 7, 1865, all in Correspondance Houzeau-Schmit; Houzeau to his parents, July 23, 1865, in Houzeau Papers.

French-language section would be to maintain the unity of ideas
and policy in the center of the directing group, while the English-
language section would deal with the outside world. The latter
would be our major weapon of attack and defense; and thus it demanded the most attention and care.

The second obstacle to this Louisiana group becoming the
spokesman and guide for the masses of African descent was the
alienation of the black slave from the free man of color. There
were reasons, it must be admitted, for this alienation. Many free
men of color had succumbed to the weakness of owning slaves
themselves.[35] They tended to separate their struggle from that of
the Negroes; some believed that they would achieve their cause
more quickly if they abandoned the black to his fate. In their eyes,
they were nearer to the white man; they were more advanced than
the slave in all respects. They believed they might be granted
what, in their opinion, the black man would never possess—civil
equality.[36] A strange error in a society in which prejudice weighed
equally against all those who had African blood in their veins, no
matter how small the amount![37] A glaring error in a country

35. In 1830 there were over 3,600 free Negro slaveowners in the United States.
Louisiana, with nearly 1,000, had far more than any other state. Carter G. Wood-
son, *Free Negro Owners of Slaves in the United States in 1830 Together with Absentee
Ownership of Slaves in the United States in 1830* (1924; New York, 1968), 1–42.
36. Free coloreds initially excluded ex-slaves from their campaign to obtain the
franchise. See David C. Rankin, "The Politics of Caste: Free Colored Leadership
in New Orleans During the Civil War," in Robert R. Macdonald, John R. Kemp,
and Edward F. Haas (eds.), *Louisiana's Black Heritage* (New Orleans, 1979),
125–38.
37. In a letter outlining the absurdities of race prejudice in New Orleans,
Houzeau wrote, "I cannot refrain from laughing when I hear ladies who are blond
like Russians and pale like Hollanders called 'negresses.' I ask myself if these 'nobles' have their good sense when I see them refusing the hand of, and treating with
contempt, doctors, lawyers, and Protestant ministers who are whiter than me,
raised in France and England, and their superiors (and by a lot) in intelligence,
education, morality, and often also in wealth." Houzeau to "My Dear Friends [his
parents]," February 12, 1865, in Houzeau Papers. Houzeau's own experience in
New Orleans testifies to the social as well as the biological basis of race prejudice.
Although he had no "African blood" in his veins, Houzeau was defined as a Negro

where a man of the lightest skin color, even if he were free, was subject to the Code Noir as though he were a slave on a plantation!

Besides, what could this small body of free mulattoes have accomplished if white men had raised its status alone? It would have been lost in the masses; it would have been an unnoticeable legal minority, a minority incapable of action, without influence, condemned beforehand to having only the pretense of its rights. In contrast, by placing themselves at the head of the freed slaves, these leaders would have an army; in dealing with them, the rest of the country would have to take account of their numbers.[38] Moreover, the black man would shield the man of color. For, in case of a reaction, if the mulatto alone possessed rights, he would be struck down first, whereas after the elevation of the Negro a more violent reaction, an all-powerful and terrible reaction, would be necessary to reach the man who is almost white.

Finally, in a time of social transformation it is always an advantage to stand firmly on principle. It was easier to demand the freedom of all in the name of the Laws of Nature than the elevation of a handful of men of varying lighter shades in the name of expediency. It was necessary to invoke justice, and justice is the same for all men, whatever the shade of their skin.

Nevertheless, I had great difficulty in gaining the support of both shades and in inspiring confidence among the blacks. The light-colored men with a few exceptions were sufficiently intelligent to understand the necessity of this alliance, but the blacks continued to be distrustful. I was forced to exaggerate my support

---

because he acted like one, because his behavior, as he states in "My Passage," 83, was "so extraordinary, so exorbitant, that the only way to explain it was to imagine that I might be of African blood myself."

38. In 1860 there were in Louisiana 18,647 free Negroes, of whom 81.3 percent were of mixed ancestry, and 331,726 slaves, of whom 9.8 percent were of mixed ancestry. Bureau of the Census, *Population of the United States in 1860*, 194.

of the black party despite the possibility of losing ground among the lighter-skinned colored men. The goal, however, was too important for me to equivocate. When necessity required, these men of light skin would rally. They were right when they said that I was more interested in the blacks than in them. Above all, I had to make myself useful to the oppressed masses. It was also necessary to form an army, and were not these intelligent and capable men of color destined to be the generals? By giving them soldiers, I was serving their hopes and legitimate ambitions in the most useful fashion.

But at its beginning the *Tribune* was as yet nothing. It was not only stifled by a conspiracy of silence; there was also a conspiracy of scorn. It was generally agreed—and all the whites in New Orleans held it on the best faith—that blacks or whites "lowly enough to associate with blacks" were intrinsically worthless. And because I alone, all alone at first, among the white population took up the pen in behalf of the blacks, I forfeited my "Caucasian character," as it was called in the slang. I was dead, more than dead even, vilified in the eyes of my race. The defiant stance that I took was so extraordinary, so exorbitant, that the only way to explain it was to imagine that I might be of African blood myself. People noticed that I used the pronoun *we* in speaking of the oppressed race. Did I not have the right, like a lawyer at the bar, to identify myself with those whose rights I was defending? Yet to the last, these whites sought to avoid what might lead them to confusion by measuring me by their own standards. By supposing me black, they minimized the moral courage that I demonstrated in attacking an entire society and in taking a truly unique stand in the southern states.[39] But I never sought to deny the rumor that I

39. *I am well aware of the courageous way in which Henry Train, Judge Fisk, Anthony Fernandez, De Petitville, Flanders, and a few others had given their support to the "black newspaper." But these citizens had remained separate from their friends of color. They helped from the outside. I, alone, stood among them.*—Houzeau. Henry Train and Josiah Fisk

had African blood in my veins, because this belief helped to increase the confidence that the colored race had in me. The enemy had helped me when he thought only to injure me.

Moreover, the members of such ignorant communities, crippled by slavery, are incapable of judging a man. When skin color becomes the chief criterion, everything becomes a matter of etiquette; nothing beyond that is noticed. For a short while, families who were very interested in me—but would not have permitted this "ignorant Dalloz," the editor of the *Tribune*, to touch the soles of their shoes—received, cultivated, and entertained me as a "member of a European Academy." This dual life did not suit me, and I quickly put an end to it. But this experience proved oddly stimulating. What opinion can a man who has lived through such an experience have of those who, without knowing it, held two so different opinions of him? What value can I place today on the opinions of most men, and of what value are their most pleasing phrases and their most bitter criticisms to me any more?

When I joined the *Tribune*, we were considered nothing, or less than nothing, in New Orleans—a newspaper without a name, without influence, without value.[40] If we held our head high in the face of scorn and insult, it was only because we believed in our cause and the sanctity of law. Everything instructive, witty, or talented, put in the "black newspaper," was rejected by the society

---

were attorneys who advertised regularly in the *Tribune*, as did the auctioneer Anthony Fernandez. Train and Fernandez were directors of the New Orleans Freedmen's Aid Association. Léonce De Petitville was a resident of the city's third district in 1858. Benjamin F. Flanders (1816–1896) was U. S. congressman from Louisiana (1862–1863), military governor of Louisiana (1867–1868), and mayor of New Orleans (1870–1872). *Tribune*, July 28 (French ed.), May 13, July 2, 1865; *Gardner & Wharton's New Orleans Directory, for the Year 1858* . . . (New Orleans, 1857), 93; *Biographical Directory of the American Congress, 1774–1971* (Washington, D.C., 1971), 949.

40. Some New Orleans newspapers, including the *Times* and the *Era*, had recognized the *Tribune*'s value prior to Houzeau's arrival. *Tribune*, October 4, 1864.

in which we lived, whereas the most stupid argument by a "Caucasian" writer was admired and praised to the skies. The inhabitants were so open about this double standard, were so natural and naïve in this prejudice, that the situation was comical. They would have repeated, without appreciating the irony, the lesson taught by Mercury to Sosia: [41]

> When in high rank we have the good fortune to appear,
> Whatever we say is always good and beautiful;
> Depending upon our situation,
> Things have a way of changing names.

Yet those who trust in such a rule expose themselves to committing more than one error and prepare themselves consequently for more than one deception. A chance event soon confounded the slaveholders by putting us in the spotlight not simply before the city of New Orleans but before the entire thirty million inhabitants of the nation.

An Irishman named Michael Gleason had thrown a young black man, Joseph Hamilton,[42] into the Mississippi, and he had prevented other blacks, who had run out onto the wharf, from pulling the victim from death. This was not an act of personal vengeance, but of racial vengeance. Gleason, who was white, had drowned Hamilton, whom he had never seen and who had not spoken to him, for the simple pleasure of drowning a black man. This was a doubly odious crime. The accused was brought before the criminal court. The procedure followed the then-existing law: the jury was chosen among whites only, but black witnesses were allowed—this was

41. The lesson was actually taught by Mercury to Night in Molière's 1668 adaption of Plautus' *Amphitruo. Amphitryon: Three Plays in New Verse Translations,* trans. and ed. James H. Mantinband and Charles E. Passage (Chapel Hill, 1974), 136.

42. The thirteen-year-old boy was named Johnny Hamilton, and on December 13, 1864, even the *Picayune* expressed some sympathy for the boy and his family. See also *Tribune,* December 15, 1864.

the first step on the road to reform, since a few months earlier blacks had not been permitted to testify when the accused was white. In this case it happened that the only eyewitnesses were of the African race. Their testimony, however, was clear, positive, and consistent; moreover, the accused did not deny it. Lynch,[43] the district attorney, prosecuted with all the fervor that he drew from the facts of the case. But the proslavery jury, indignant at the idea that a white man, "a Caucasian," might be found guilty by the testimony of black or colored men, disregarded it and speedily acquitted the defendant. This annulled, in effect, the efforts of those who had worked to permit blacks to testify; it threw them aside with the most glaring injustice and partiality.

I wrote in the English section of the *Tribune* an article entitled "Is There Any Justice for the Black?"[44] In it I discussed the acquittal in the most moderate language. I reviewed the principles on which the jury system is based, and set forth the guarantees that it was supposed to offer. I described on one side society and its need to repress crime and avenge innocence, and on the other the accused with his right to an impartial judgment of his acts. It is not only a matter of choosing a jury "from the locality," as the English law states, but also of choosing it impartially from all classes of society. What happens to these guarantees if the jury is all of one caste, of one race, in a country where two different races exist and where one of them believes that it has complete dominion over the other?

I wrote this article under the impulse of strong emotion, but the

43. Bartholomew L. Lynch was attorney general of the state of Louisiana, 1864–1865. Born in Ireland, he settled in New Orleans in 1855 and was admitted to the bar in 1857. He testified in 1866 that a Union man would have "a very poor chance" of getting a fair trial in Louisiana "in consequence of the formation of the jury." The officials picking jurors were all ex-Confederates, according to Lynch. *House Reports*, 39th Cong., 2nd Sess., No. 16, *Report of the Select Committee on the New Orleans Riots* (1867) (cited hereinafter as *New Orleans Riots*), 238–40.

44. *Tribune*, December 15, 1864. For a negative reaction to the article and Houzeau's rebuttal, see *ibid.*, December 20, 1864.

question was too clear, the truth too striking, for me not to gain real advantages in presenting it. Several days after its publication, a congressman from Pennsylvania, Mr. Kelley,[45] one of the most important leaders of the liberal party, raised the question in the House of Representatives. After reminding his audience that the New Orleans *Tribune*, "founded and edited by men of color," was dedicated to the defense of the oppressed race, this representative from Philadelphia referred to my article in words too flattering to be cited here; he then read a long passage whose ideas he supported with all the authority of his talent and position.[46]

This was a sort of baptism for the *Tribune*. From this day on, we stood before the nation. We had the right to tell the supporters of slavery in New Orleans who had believed that they would smother us through their scorn, "We do not write for you; we have a better educated and more elevated public." Had our neighbor, the white press, which published thousands of copies and

45. William D. Kelley (1814–1890) was born in Philadelphia. First elected to the House of Representatives as a Republican in 1860, he was subsequently reelected fourteen times. Kelley was an early and eloquent advocate of the abolition of slavery and the extension of full civil and political equality to the freedmen. Ira V. Brown, "William D. Kelley and Radical Reconstruction," *Pennsylvania Magazine of History and Biography*, LXXXV (1961), 316–29.

46. Before quoting Houzeau's editorial, Kelley stated: "I find in the New Orleans *Tribune* of December 15, 1864, which paper, I may remark, is the organ of the proscribed race in Louisiana, and is owned and edited and printed daily in the French and English language by persons of that race, an admirable article in response to the question, 'Is there any justice for the black?'" The speech, which received such widespread notoriety that half a million copies of it were printed, was probably the most influential one of Kelley's distinguished career. Houzeau wrote in the *Tribune* about Kelley quoting him and told his Belgian friends about it, too. Kelley probably knew about Houzeau's editorial because on the day it appeared the influential Louisiana Unionist Thomas J. Durant wrote to the publisher of the *Tribune*: "It is important that the article of this morning on the infamous Gleason case should go to leading senators and representatives in Washington." *Congressional Globe*, 38th Cong., 2nd Sess., 289; Brown, "Kelley," 321; *Tribune*, February 10, 1865; Houzeau to N. C. Schmit, February 18, 1865, in Correspondance Houzeau-Schmit; Durant to J. B. Roudanez, December 15, 1864, in Thomas J. Durant Papers, New-York Historical Society, New York.

which was infatuated with its local popularity, ever published an article where the great political and social issues were treated in the same manner as the new question now put before the Congress? It was only a bought press, furnishing, according to the American expression, "marketable merchandise." It never contained anything that its supporters, its friends in the national assembly, could take up and read before the entire nation.

Instead of showing judgment, practical sense, and moderation, these newspapers decided to flatter the pride of the planters; and far from making them aware of their true situation, encouraged them in their folly. Slavery distorts and corrupts all that it touches. This press, almost without exception, was nothing but a press of sycophants. Instinctively, it followed the rule of conduct so well expressed by the fable writer:[47]

> Amuse the "great" with dreams,
> Flatter them, feed them agreeable lies:
> Whatever the indignation that fills their hearts,
> They will swallow the bait; you will be their friend.

This lying press precipitated and multiplied the problems; it ruined the planters who, had they been well advised, would have obtained an ample reimbursement for their slaves before the war.[48] It encouraged resistance and bred anger when it was futile and all hope was lost. It drove the slaveowners from one mistake to another; these mistakes brought about a social transformation—each eliciting a protest from the nation and, consequently,

47. Probably the eighteenth-century French fabulist Jean-Pierre Claris de Florian.

48. Compensated emancipation was never seriously considered in antebellum Louisiana. Lincoln advocated federal compensation during the Civil War, but with the exception of the District of Columbia his plan was never implemented. J. G. Randall and David Donald, *The Civil War and Reconstruction* (Lexington, Mass., 1969), 372–75.

advancing the cause of liberty by a step. How many times have I had occasion to thank this press for being constantly false to its mission, for being flattering, deceitful, and mercenary!

The *Tribune* took a totally different path. The more the press of the "superior race" resorted to empty rhetoric, the more I myself desired to sustain not only a dignified tone but a high level of thought for "the Negro newspaper." I enjoyed by means of this contrast exposing the mediocrity of these arrogant newspapers. To serve the "planters' market," the editors of these newspapers did not need much knowledge or instruction. I liked to quote works of political economy and technology in the *Tribune* in order to let the experts in these disciplines condemn to silence the errors published the day before in proslavery articles. I cited historical narratives, often taken word-for-word from famous books, in order to refute the blunders that they had made.[49] I would even quote, in connection with their articles, passages from English and Latin classics, which supported their own theses but which they were too ignorant to cite. I did this to make them feel their literary inferiority, whatever their "racial superiority."

Often, I drew parallels between historical events and the current political situation: for example, there were striking similarities between the southern planters and the French *émigrés* of 1792. Like the *émigrés*, the slaveholders had revolted against their country in the hope of saving institutions that the country no longer wanted and whose natural term had arrived. Like them, they nourished themselves with illusions and vowed to learn nothing, and to forget nothing. Just as the noble *émigrés* deceived themselves in the hope of regaining their lost goods and privileges, the

---

49. See, for example, the way in which Houzeau attacks the flattering depiction of southern planters in the white press by drawing upon the works of Basil Hall, Harriet Martineau, Captain Frederick Marryat, and Frederick Law Olmsted. *Tribune*, July 2, 1865.

American planters never doubted that they would regain their slaves. But when peace came, the *biens nationaux* had been sold. The land had already changed hands; it had passed to a totally new class that could not be ruined merely by sheer wantonness. Feudal rights had fallen forever.[50] In the same way, the blacks of the United States were to leave the plantations; soon they would acquire possessions, create their own culture, and set up institutions. Each month, each day that passed, brought about the new order of things. How could things ever be reversed? The situation of the planters and that of the *émigrés*, their illusions, their hatred of the "usurper," presented very striking analogies.

Indeed, there were numerous other historical situations from the last two centuries that furnished illuminating insights into the events at hand. I had made a detailed study of the three great states, France, England, and the United States, during the preceding one hundred fifty years; and I repeatedly found occasion to cite curious and instructive incidents.[51]

Don't you see, I said, that civilized societies are not static? Nations move forward and undergo change. Clearly the France of

50. The émigrés of 1792 were members of the French nobility who fled their homeland to join counterrevolutionary forces headed by European powers in the hope of overthrowing the revolutionary régime and restoring the monarchy. Their lands, along with those held by the clergy, were confiscated by the revolutionary government and became part of the *biens nationaux*, or national property, which was sold to finance the Revolution. Houzeau also compared the persecution of freedmen in rural Louisiana during Reconstruction with the bloodbath in the Gironde region of France following the restoration of the monarchy in 1814–1815. Georges Lefebvre, *The French Revolution from Its Origins to 1873*, trans. Elizabeth M. Evanson (New York, 1962), 192–95; Lefebvre, *The French Revolution from 1793 to 1799*, trans. John H. Stewart and James Friguglietti (New York, 1964), 47–48, 56, 111–12; "La terreur blanche," *Tribune*, August 3, 1865 (French ed.).

51. See, for example, *Tribune*, February 23, March 8, May 30, June 7 (French ed.), 9, 27, 1865, September 23 (French ed.), October 19 (French ed.), 1866, October 29 (French ed.), 31 (French ed.), November 29 (French ed.), 1867. Houzeau also made frequent reference to conditions in contemporary Europe; he even reprinted articles from Belgian newspapers in the *Tribune*. See, for example, *ibid.*, June 23, 1867 (French ed.).

Louis XV was not that of Louis XIV. That of Louis XVI was again different from that of Louis XV, and the France of Louis XVIII instead of reproducing that of Louis XVI was far different. Even the France of Louis-Philippe was no longer that of Charles X; and how the Second Empire differs from the First! Everything changes, everything restructures itself; this is the veritable life of nations. Those who stand against the natural flow of events only prove their ignorance. When an institution is falling, those who hang on merely fall with it.

How can you hope to save slavery and the Code Noir! Is there no solidarity among civilized nations? Don't commercial relations, travel, newspapers, books, which today link all regions, create a kind of unity in spite of you? The result of this unity is to introduce a like spirit, a like character, into society at large. Italy attempted to close its borders to the railroad: a pontifical bull of 1839 had forbidden it to enter its territory. But did not the railroad force the pope to retreat, and has it not in fact even pushed into Roman territory?[52] Who can ban the steam engine or even chemical matches? Well, there are moral ideas that are as powerful as these material instruments of society. When sorcery disappeared from one state, it soon disappeared from all other states. When absolute government yielded to limited government, this reform spread throughout Europe. Once elections were introduced, this innovation gradually spread everywhere. And in legislation, be it civil, commercial, or criminal, there is similar progress among all enlightened peoples. These parallel changes prove the unity of ideas. No civilized nation can remove itself from this influence. In summary, the maintenance of a caste system and, more than that even, of slavery is in discord with civilization today. Should the

52. On the opposition of Pope Gregory XVI (1765–1846) to the construction of railroads in the Papal States, see Pietro Negri, "Gregorio XVI e le ferrovie," *Rasségna degli Archivi di Stato*, XXVIII (1968), 103–26.

southern states congratulate themselves for alone opposing the great liberal movement? They are the last, or nearly so, to consider reform;[53] as time passes, the pressure becomes increasingly great to do so. If resistance is successful today, this will not prevent it from failing tomorrow. What does one gain by being blind? The fall is all the more dangerous and damaging, and the disappointment all the deeper.

These were the main ideas that I presented at that time, ideas that would have led only to peace and conciliation as long as the rights acquired by the newly freed masses were respected. By the end of 1864, one could clearly see that slavery could not survive the crisis that now confronted the nation.[54] Lincoln's proclamation was becoming a reality, albeit slowly. Emancipation was still partial; it had only begun to be implemented behind Federal lines; yet the status of the African race after its emancipation had already become an issue. There was a tendency to transform slaves into pariahs, that is to say, to leave them midway, making them neither citizens nor even men. "It is enough to free them," people said; "let them be free as the beasts in the fields." To do this was to stop short of facing the consequences of emancipation. It was necessary to combat this attitude which, leaving aside its injustice, was full of danger for the nation.[55]

First, it was necessary to refute the erroneous belief that the black or colored man was in all cases inferior to the white. This proposition had gained acceptance in men's minds thanks to the biased descriptions of the slavemasters whose word the northern

53. Slavery was not completely abolished in Puerto Rico until 1873, in Cuba until 1886, and in Brazil until 1888.

54. Houzeau believed that Lincoln's reelection in November, 1864, would result in the abolition of slavery. Houzeau to his father, October 18, 1864, Houzeau to his mother, November 22, 1864, in Houzeau Papers.

55. On early federal policy toward the freedmen, see Louis S. Gerteis, *From Contraband to Freedman: Federal Policy Toward Southern Blacks, 1861–1865* (Westport, Conn., 1973).

public readily believed since they were in a better position to judge. But it was in the slaveowners' best interest to mislead, a fact that the public did not take into account. If one were to state that the median of development is not the same among all human races, nor among all people, this would only state an observable fact. If one were to add that for the blacks from the backward regions of Africa or from the plantations of the southern United States, where they were deliberately kept in ignorance, the median is below that of civilized whites, one would still be perfectly correct. But it would be absurd to conclude from this that without exception all individuals who have African blood in their veins are inferior, are destined to be inferior, to the most brutish and degraded white men. Once one leaves medians to pass to individuals, we find that each race has its own chain of characteristics and developments, and that the head of the black or colored series unquestionably surpasses the bottom of the white or "Caucasian" series. To say that there is no white cretin who is inferior to the American Frederick Douglass[56] or to Alexandre Dumas[57] would make oneself look ridiculous in every country save that of slavery. How many times have I seen a Caucasian gentleman fall drunk into a gutter in New Orleans, sprawled, as Shakespeare would have said, in his own vomit? The decent black servant, sober, properly dressed, would come by; recognizing the white man, he

56. Frederick Douglass (1817–1895), the most famous Afro-American of the Civil War era, was born a slave in Maryland. After escaping from slavery in 1838, he became a leading abolitionist, journalist, and orator. During Reconstruction Douglass visited New Orleans and was greatly impressed with the Negro leaders he encountered there. Benjamin Quarles, *Frederick Douglass* (Washington, D.C., 1948); *Louisianian*, May 11, 1872.

57. Alexandre Dumas (1802–1870), one of the giants of nineteenth-century French literature, was the grandson of a Saint Dominguan Negro. Among his more important works are the plays *Henri III et sa cour* (1829) and *Antony* (1831), and the novels *Le Comte de Monte-Cristo* (1844–45) and *Les trois mousquetaires* (1844). Altogether his works filled 103 volumes. Sir Paul Harvey and J. E. Heseltine (comps. and eds.), *The Oxford Companion to French Literature* (Oxford, 1959), 232–33.

would help him get up and would take him to his own home. Which man in this case was the superior, which the inferior?

The same thing could be said of the white tramp compared to the working man of color, of the white libertine compared to the black man of temperate life, of the white thief and assassin compared to the honest and virtuous black man. Each day current events gave me the chance to refute the lie of absolute white superiority. My portraits of morality in action enraged the slaveholders who secretly were eager to read the *Tribune*, if only to tear it to shreds while reading it.

In fact, we cannot establish rules governing the relative situation of races, nor nations, nor provinces, nor families according to considerations of medians and averages—this would be grossly unfair. It is wonderful to be a descendant of the prophet Mohammed and to wear a green turban, which gives one the right to certain privileges.[58] But is this the principle of modern society? We proclaim that each person is the product of his own deeds and only responsible for his own actions; the sins of the fathers, we believe today, should never fall upon their children. "Would any state," Cicero has already asked, "tolerate a lawgiver who should enact that a son or grandson was to be sentenced for the transgression of a father or grandfather?"[59]

It is thus absurd to speak of privileges or proscriptions that are transmitted by parentage. The legislator can only deal with individuals; it is necessary to take each of these for what he is worth. Let all men have the same rights in a society, and then each one, whatever his color, will be able to find his true place.

58. The green turban is the well-known badge of the descendants of the Prophet Mohammed; it has also, however, been adopted by other groups of Moslems who claim no direct relation to the Prophet. M. T. Houtsma *et al.* (eds.), *The Encyclopaedia of Islam* (4 vols.; Leyden, 1908–34), IV, 886–87.

59. Cicero, *De natura deorum academica*, trans. H. Rackham (London, 1933), 377.

But aside from this question of principle that concerns the future of the United States, especially the development of its democratic institutions, there was a question of national interest, more likely perhaps to stimulate the minds of Americans: this was the need to unify the country. As long as the two races remained separate, two types of schools would exist in which children would be brought up in two distinct groups, and two types of churches— or churches with divided seating; as long as prejudice and discrimination were maintained, the two elements would necessarily be at odds. Two peoples were being created, instead of one.[60] But any area inhabited by two distinct peoples lacks national unity, internal vigor, and strength against foreigners. It is the homogeneity of peoples that is the source of their power. To exclude one-sixth of the population is to weaken oneself foolishly.[61] This error is all the more evident when the element excluded is one that is completely patriotic and loyal, and when the one included (the southern whites) belongs to a class recently in revolt and still today discontented, subversive, and dangerous. The United States is a great hospitable land open to immigrants of all nations.[62] May it be the common land where not only all the white people will melt

60. In an editorial advocating the desegregation of New Orleans public schools, Houzeau wrote in the *Tribune* of May 9, 1867: "We have to make this community one nation and one people, where two nations and two people previously existed. We had better begin at the root, and first of all unite the children in the public schools."

61. *Today there are 58 million whites (Anglo-Saxons, Germans, Latins, and Slavs), 5 million blacks and men of mixed blood, 500,000 Chinese, and 500,000 Indians and mestizos of mixed red and white blood.*—HOUZEAU. Actually, the population of the United States in 1870 was 33,589,377 whites; 4,880,009 Negroes; 63,254 Chinese and Japanese; and 25,731 Indians. Bureau of the Census, *Statistics of the Population of the United States at the Tenth Census (June 1, 1880)* . . . (Washington, D.C., 1883), 378–79.

62. Houzeau later warned Europeans that adjustment to life in America could be difficult, and he advised those encouraging emigration to do so with "very great prudence." See his "L'Amérique et l'émigration," which appears as a foreword to A. Lancaster, *Quatre mois au Texas: Notes de voyage* (Mons, 1887), 5–23.

together but also all races—the "Caucasian," the black represented by the African, the yellow Chinese, and the red Indian. This destiny is implied even by the composition of the population itself. It is important to bind these diverse elements together, to make them into a whole, a union, a nation. To leave several groups without caste is to weaken the state for the future. Give us equality before the law, equality in schooling, equality in public hiring, and you will have one indivisible people; and by the year 1900, when your population will be in the hundred millions and you will have formed the most powerful agglomeration that civilization has ever known, you will constitute a unified and great nation.

I can only mention the plan of attack that I followed in 1865 and 1866 very briefly here. These steps led to great developments. The North, in the end, was not unfeeling despite the prejudiced views communicated to it. The *Tribune*, said the Philadelphia lawyer Hornor,[63] is the drop of water that is wearing away the rock. But at that time we had in the abolitionist press, the special press of the North, some helpers who, without dealing with these questions from the same point of view, had begun nonetheless to clear the way.

For the men of color, the first course of action was to demand their rights as free men by all the means permitted under the law. The population of African race had already had its meetings in Louisiana; in January, 1865, it decided to hold a convention. Delegates came to it from all parts of the state.[64] The issue at hand was

63. Charles W. Hornor, law partner of Thomas J. Durant, was a radical white Unionist who opposed as too moderate the 1864 state constitution drawn up in accordance with Lincoln's plan of reconstruction. He later served as an officer of the New Orleans Freedmen's Aid Association. *Tribune*, August 18, 1864, May 2, 1865.

64. This was the Convention of Colored Men of Louisiana, which met in New Orleans on January 9–14, 1865. An analysis of the lists of delegates published in the *Tribune*, January 10, 11, 12, 13, 14, 1865 (French and English eds.), reveals that

to reach agreement on a course of action to bring about the great principle of equality before the law. This convention, or rather this congress as one would call it in Europe, lasted one week and was remarkable in the practicality, the order, and the firmness that it showed. Among the French-speaking delegates were many educated and energetic men, but since it was necessary to speak English, they were necessarily relegated to minor roles. Among the English-speaking element, one man shone forth above all others: Captain James Ingraham.[65] He had served in a black regiment of the Federal army and had distinguished himself at Port Hudson.[66] Those who witnessed him at this convention, those who have followed his efforts to deal with these problems on the largest possible scale and in the broadest possible way, those who heard his untutored but vigorous and fiery eloquence, will always honor him whatever were his later waverings and mistakes.[67] He was, keeping due proportion in mind, the Mirabeau of the men of color in Louisiana, Mirabeau before his alliance with the court.[68]

---

only seven parishes other than Orleans were represented at the convention, and over 85 percent of the delegates were from Orleans.

65. James H. Ingraham, a carpenter, was born in Mississippi in 1833, the son of a white man and a slave. Freed when only six years old, Ingraham later enrolled in the Louisiana Native Guards and fought at the battle for Port Hudson. He served in the Louisiana state senate from 1870–1874. Ingraham was involved in a graft scandal in 1876, and he died sometime prior to 1879, when money was being raised for his impoverished widow. *Tribune*, May 14, 1865; *National Republican*, January 2, 1872; *Times*, February 2, 3, March 9, 1876; *Louisianian*, May 3, 1879; Charles Vincent, *Black Legislators in Louisiana During Reconstruction* (Baton Rouge, 1976), 8, 236; Rankin, "Origins of Negro Leadership," 157, 184.

66. Port Hudson, a strategic fort on the Mississippi River, fell to Union forces, including two Negro regiments from Louisiana, in July, 1863. For a discussion of Afro-American participation in the battle for Port Hudson, see William F. Messner, *Freedmen and the Ideology of Free Labor: Louisiana, 1862–1865* (Lafayette, La., 1978), 132–37.

67. Ingraham, much to the *Tribune*'s disgust, later aligned himself with the moderate wing of the Republican party headed by the carpetbagger Henry Clay Warmoth. *Republican*, December 8, 29, 1867, March 20, 1868; F. Wayne Binning, "Carpetbaggers' Triumph: The Louisiana State Election of 1868," *Louisiana History*, XIV (1973), 21–39.

68. Count Honoré de Mirabeau (1749–1791) was a renegade nobleman and

The question that stirred the assembly was whether it should address the state legislature or the United States Congress to establish the groundwork for the new order of things. According to the ideas expressed by the *Tribune*, to address the state authorities would be useless.[69] Even though the state legislature at that time had liberal tendencies, it lacked the courage to initiate social reform opposed by its constituents—the whites. If it wanted colored men to seek it out, it was only in order to create clients among them. But the petition would have remained without effect. Even if colored men had obtained a few rights through state legislation, were not these laws subject to recall by a subsequent legislature? And, moreover, what a strange state of affairs would be created if such rights depended on the goodwill of individual states—the man of African race having only certain rights in Louisiana, certain others in Georgia, certain others in Carolina, and all this without coordination, without unity. The black permitted to own land in Mississippi might see himself losing this right while traveling through Alabama or Virginia. In one place he could testify in court, in the other he could not; on one bank of the Mississippi he could be a pilot, on the other he could be sent to jail for piloting a boat. What was needed was a single rule so that one would know where one stood. It was not the southerners, narrow and mean in their state governments, but the nation, through its congressional representatives in Washington, who ought to decide these great questions concerning the new life.

The colored convention understood this, and it eventually de-

---

eloquent spokesman for the Third Estate during the early days of the French Revolution. He tried to mediate between the king and the National Assembly and ultimately went over completely to the king. Lefebvre, *French Revolution From Its Origins*, 175–76.

69. The *Tribune* did not take a stand on the issue of whether the convention should petition the state legislature or Congress until after the convention had voted on the issue. Then the *Tribune* vigorously supported the convention's decision to petition Congress. *Tribune*, January 17, 22, 24, 1865.

cided to seek help from the United States Congress. But the stealthy efforts of certain whites,[70] above all those who sought to turn the African population into submissive, obsequious clients, were able momentarily to divide the assembly. It was at this point that Captain Ingraham made use of all his energy and convinced the majority to return to his view.[71]

The situation had not developed, however, to the point that the Congress of the United States felt obliged to intervene. All the energy of the central government continued to be directed toward the successful conclusion of the armed conflict.[72] The first goal, in effect, was to defeat the proslavery *Vendée*,[73] and to affirm the government's jurisdiction. But just at this time the occupation of Richmond occurred, followed quickly by the surrender of General Lee.[74] The war was over. The last word of "secession" had just been spoken. All that remained for the South, now wide open before the conqueror, was to carry out its own execution by emancipating its slaves. An amendment to the Federal Constitution, known as the Thirteenth Amendment, generalized the abolition of

70. Shortly after the convention adjourned, the *Tribune* chided these "white wire-pullers": "At the first step . . . that we attempt to make, we find tutors around us, who take upon themselves to redress our conduct, and try to prescribe what we have to do. . . . We need friends, it is true; but we do not need tutors. The age of guardianship is past forever." *Tribune*, January 20, February 10, 1865.

71. Ingraham grandly advised the convention: "It is not before them [state legislators], but before the world, that we have to lay our claims." *Tribune*, January 14, 1865.

72. Through the Confiscation Act of July, 1862, the Freedmen's Bureau Bill of March, 1865, etc., Congress had prior to the close of civil war become involved in the process of reconstruction. In fact, Louisiana was the stimulus for much congressional thought and action. See Herman Belz, *Reconstructing the Union: Theory and Policy During the Civil War* (Ithaca, N.Y., 1969); McCrary, *Abraham Lincoln*, chs. 2–10.

73. The Vendée was a revolt of peasants, rural artisans, priests, and nobles in western France against the revolutionary government of 1793. Although it took the form of renewed royalism, the revolt was largely the result of local grievances. See Charles Tilly, *The Vendée* (Cambridge, Mass., 1964).

74. Union forces occupied Richmond on April 3, 1865, and Lee surrendered on April 9.

slavery, which had hitherto been only partially accomplished by legislation whose constitutionality could be questioned. With the Thirteenth Amendment, slavery was abolished as a general principle throughout the United States, and the power to reestablish it was taken away from the states.[75] Thus were the words that I had written in 1862 justified: "This war will be called by history the war for the suppression of slavery."[76] This is very much the way we see things today when we look back from a broad perspective at the war and what it produced.

The further we get from these events, the more secondary incidents fade, leaving us only two great facts—planters fighting to assure the continuation of servitude in their domain, and the defeat of these slaveholders, bringing with it as an inevitable consequence the emancipation of the blacks. So the period that followed, which has already lasted more than five years, is one devoted to the work of building schools, extending education among the freed slaves, guaranteeing blacks their civil rights, and introducing them to politics. The entire effort of the United States is focused on the mighty task of raising up and assimilating a previously separate population. One great concern, a single and abiding concern dominated this gigantic crisis—to end the oppression that weighed on the blacks.

But what appears certain today was contested, even insistently denied, at the beginning and during the course of the war. I hope that you will pardon me for reprinting here a passage from a letter that I wrote to one of my European critics in November, 1863. Although this was a personal letter, a letter to a friend, I kept a

75. The Thirteenth Amendment abolishing slavery was ratified on December 18, 1865.

76. Houzeau, *Question de l'esclavage*, 215. In the final paragraph of this work (p. 216), Houzeau wrote of the Civil War: "Again, it is not a problem of economics or of the organization of agricultural labor that is being agitated; the question is more elevated and more general: the North and South are debating the cause of human liberty."

copy, contrary to my habit, so confident was I that events would bear me out some day. "I well know," I wrote,

> that I have drawn as much blame upon myself as my small being can bear through my first paltry sketches of slavery. . . . A sizable industry, the cotton industry, was so to speak destroyed; commercial relations were deeply affected; the jealousy of a few great powers dangled the hope of diplomatic recognition before the eyes of the South, which only doubled its bitterness. I am not at all surprised then to have the whole world against me. Nevertheless, I am not going to give up. The time will come when people will realize that I was right. The clamor of special interests will cease, the sentiments of jealous men will no longer find an object; and the false colors will have fallen. When this occurs, slavery itself will have disappeared. Then we shall see nothing more than the justice of emancipation and its advantages. No one will remember that he questioned its legitimacy, or lacked confidence in its supporters, or encouraged its adversaries. No one, among the generation that will follow ours, will understand how impartial spectators could be divided on a question for which the lessons of education, the illumination of science, the natural movement of the heart, permit only one possible solution. It will then be said: "The matter was so simple; it could not have been otherwise."[77]

Was I not right to keep a copy of these words? What happened to the Latin empire in Mexico? Where is the Southern Confederacy today? Who still hopes to see the United States divided?

---

77. *Letter to Captain A . . . of the General Staff of the Belgian Army.*—HOUZEAU. Captain A is the Belgian cartographer Émile H. J. Adan (1830–1882). Houzeau's letters to Adan have not been found. See Herman V. Linden, "Émile-Henri-Joseph Adan," in the Belgian *Biographie nationale*, XXIX, supplément 1 (1956), 21–25.

These dreams have passed like fleeting images, leaving hardly a
memory behind,

> And, like an insubstantial pageant faded,
> Leave not a rack behind. . . .[78]

Only one thing remained as the consequence of all these
events, the abolition of slavery, and even more than the abolition,
the development of its logical consequences. For we are far from
the days when the freedman was nothing more than "contraband"[79] and cannon fodder. It is with difficulty that we remember
having discussed seriously whether the black should have schools,
whether he should have his civil rights recognized, and whether he
should be a member of the political body of the state. Today members of his race sit in the Congress of the United States!

Hence it was now the great task of social integration that was
to follow the crises of abolition. The first phase, that of emancipation properly speaking, was over. A new question arose, more
important perhaps than that of emancipation, a question more difficult to solve and which required greater abilities among politicians and statesmen: what would be the status of the population
of African descent? Would we leave it suspended between liberty
and virility, if I dare express myself in this way? Would it be considered a legal minor as women are? Would it become a class of
serfs, bound to the soil? Would it be ruled by special laws, by a
modified Code Noir? No! Equity and the character of American
institutions demanded that it be admitted to the main body of the

78. Shakespeare, *The Tempest*, Act IV, scene 1.
79. In May, 1861, Benjamin F. Butler, commanding general at Fort Monroe,
Virginia, refused to release fugitive Negro slaves who had crossed behind Union
lines. He declared that they were contraband, or property useful to the enemy, and
thus liable to confiscation by the laws of war. The term originally applied to slaves
captured by Union military forces, but increasingly was used as a slang word to
refer to Negroes generally. Gerteis, *Contraband to Freedman*, 11–32.

nation. There remained but one obstacle—prejudice; but it was an obstacle of immense power. Almost all public officials lacked the necessary moral courage to attack it head on. A few even shared in this regrettable error.[80]

In the spring of 1865, at a time when plantation work was in abeyance since the new agricultural year was about to begin, General Hurlbut, then military commander of Louisiana, issued regulations concerning agricultural labor.[81] Well, these regulations were nothing other than slavery in a thinly disguised form. The worker had to hire himself out for a year; he could not leave the plantation without a permit from his master, issued by the military authorities.[82] And since it was impossible to distinguish between a plantation worker and a craftsman or professional by sight, it was necessary in order to make the measure effective to require the "circulation card" of all those who had black or brown skin. Consequently, merchants, doctors, businessmen, if they were black or brown, could no longer leave the city or freely travel from town to town. This put the former free black in a worse situation than the one he had suffered under the Code Noir.

80. For a brief but illuminating discussion of racism among northern politicians, see C. Vann Woodward, *American Counterpoint: Slavery and Racism in the North-South Dialogue* (Boston, 1971), 163–83.

81. Stephen A. Hurlbut (1815–1882), a native South Carolinian, was commander of the Department of the Gulf from September, 1864–April, 1865. Joseph G. Dawson III, *Army Generals and Reconstruction: Louisiana, 1862–1877* (Baton Rouge, 1982), 19–22, 266. See Hurlbut's March 11, 1865, labor regulations (General Order No. 23) in *The War of the Rebellion: A Compilation of the Official Records of the Union and Confederate Armies* (120 vols.; Washington, D.C., 1880–1901), Ser. I, XLVIII, pt. 1, pp. 1146–48.

82. Section 9 of General Order No. 23 stated that "laborers will be allowed and encouraged to choose their own employers, but when they have once selected they must fulfill their contract for the year, and will not be permitted to leave their place of employment (except in cases where they are permitted so to do for just reason, by the authority of the superintendent), and if they do so leave without cause and permission they will forfeit all wages earned to the time of abandonment and be otherwise punished, as the nature of the case may require." *Ibid.*, XLVIII, 1147.

But for the newly freed man, it was to chain him for a year to an "apprenticeship" that was in no way authorized by law. It violated the worker's right to choose his employer and to leave a master who oppressed him. Following slavery, this form of subjugation was all the more dangerous because instead of breaking with traditional errors, it perpetuated them. What became of the principle of freedom of contract if a master refused to give his workers the *permit* necessary to seek work elsewhere? Moreover, what effect did this regulation have on the right to negotiate salaries? The worker was put on a salary schedule according to whether he was *good*, *average*, or *bad*, and the employer was the judge of his abilities. The wage scale was set excessively low, and the planter had to feed and lodge his workers just as in the days of slavery.[83] He was forbidden to use corporal punishment. But what good was such a prohibition? To whom could the black man complain? He could not leave the plantation. The competent authority was not the civil tribunal (made up in any case of planters), but a regional military representative, who was regaled with festivals provided by the large landowners and who, with very few exceptions, did not wish to irritate the planters, and often could not do so without endangering himself.

Instead of establishing freedom of work, freedom of contract, freedom to negotiate salaries, frequent payment (monthly or weekly),[84] everything in this regulation was calculated to create

83. Section 5 of General Order No. 23 stated that "in addition to just treatment, wholesome rations, comfortable clothing, quarters, fuel, and medical attendance, and the opportunity for instruction of children, the planter shall pay to the laborer as follows: Male hands, first class, $10 per month; second class, $8 per month; third class, $6 per month. Female hands, first class, $8 per month; second class, $6 per month; third class, $5 per month. Boys under fourteen, $3 per month; girls under fourteen, $2 per month. These classes will be determined by merit and on agreement between the planters and the laborers." *Ibid.*

84. Under General Order No. 23 laborers were to be paid four times a year, on May 1, August 1, November 1, and on or before January 31. *Ibid.*

the least disturbance in the traditional attitudes and relationships, to maintain the absolute power of the master over the plantation worker. Under this regime, hundreds of planters were easily able to convince their workers, isolated in the countryside, "that nothing had changed." When necessary, a person would be brought in, dressed in a Federal uniform, to declare to the blacks that slavery had been reestablished. Therefore, this regulation was bad on all counts. Not only did it violate the spirit of the proclamation of January 1, 1863, which abolished slavery, but instead of preparing new pathways, it reestablished the old and thus made the later task of transformation even more difficult and arduous. It encouraged useless hopes and tyranny among the planters. It prevented the establishment of open relationships and of unconstrained movement, which are the right of the free worker. It went so far as to deny to the older blacks and colored men who had been born free the famous right, which they had always enjoyed, to come and go as they pleased.[85] From the point of view of the African race, it was iniquitous; from the point of view of economic interests, it stupidly prolonged the period of transition and crisis; finally, in the perspective of general politics and the highest concerns of the land, it was a grave mistake.

I made these truths apparent in three English-language articles that appeared in three successive issues of the *Tribune*.[86] The system was so wrong that even the general himself felt implicated. He had surrendered to the enemy, and it was thoroughly disagreeable for him to have this fact proven, I dare say, without a doubt, and this in the pages of a black newspaper to boot! The next day, he inquired about the authorship of these articles; and

85. Various laws had required free Negroes in antebellum Louisiana to carry certificates of identification when moving about, but these acts were rarely enforced. See Rankin, "Tannenbaum Thesis," 30; Sterkx, *Free Negro*, 163–64, 196.

86. *Tribune*, March 28, 29, 30, 1865. The paper had previously leveled serious criticisms of General Order No. 23 on March 14, 16, 18, 22, 1865.

learning that I was not an American, he spoke of "chasing me out of the country." It is not my place to determine which of the two of us, he or I, most usefully and faithfully served the development of American institutions, the forward political march of the United States, and its future strength and greatness. The third article appeared after this threat, and it was the bluntest of all.[87] No, I had not been thrown out, but I owed this "favor" to the echoes that my justifiable complaints found in the North. The *Anti-Slavery Standard*, the *Commonwealth*, the *Independent*,[88] the New York *Tribune*, and generally all the rest of the white abolitionist press joined together to attack this system. Those aspects of the regulation that were the most worthy of condemnation were mitigated in their application; and the following year General Baird,[89] though not doing all that he should have, nevertheless brought things closer to a system based on justice and liberty.

We were marching slowly but steadily toward progress. The terrain was gradually being cleared. There was a future in sight, and at the same time the ideas of the white population, at least in the North, were changing little by little. In the South, no one

87. Houzeau wrote in his editorial of March 30, 1865: "That . . . discrimination still lives in the prejudices and habits of thoughts of the people—of the common people—we have no cause to wonder. But that such remnants of times past—and past forever—be still observable in the writings, in the official orders, in the policy, and even in the tone . . . of Commanding Generals, we can only see with a feeling of sorrow and regret." Hurlbut survived Houzeau's editorials but not the recommendation of a special military commission that he be tried for corruption. The case was hushed up, and Hurlbut was "honorably" discharged on June 20, 1865. *Tribune*, March 30, 1865; Warner, *Generals in Blue*, 245. See also Houzeau to Victor Bouvy, May 28, 1867, in Liagre Papers.

88. The *National Anti-Slavery Standard* and the *Independent* were published in New York; the *Commonwealth* was published in Boston.

89. Absalom Baird (1824–1905), a Pennsylvanian and graduate of West Point, served briefly as commander of the Department of the Gulf in the summer of 1866. He had previously been assistant commissioner of the Freedmen's Bureau in Louisiana. Though a much more radical commissioner than his predecessor J. S. Fullerton, Baird still came under attack from the *Tribune* for being too timid. *Tribune*, December 20, 1865; Dawson, *Army Generals*, 37–38; Howard A. White, *The Freedmen's Bureau in Louisiana* (Baton Rouge, 1970), 24–25.

wanted to listen to us yet; but it had become necessary to look the
situation in the face, and those who were prejudiced said, "Well! if
the black isn't a slave any more, we must get rid of him. We went
to fetch him in Africa; now we should send him out of our country." There was no great danger in letting this idea be discussed,
for its impossibility would become obvious on the day it was to be
implemented. How many ships would have been needed to transport five million people? Where were these ships to come from?
And what would be the cost? For by taking these ships away from
general world commerce, freight rates would go up, and this
would bring about a sharp rise in the cost of exotic imported
goods all over the world. Can you imagine the tonnage that
would be taken over by the needs of such a deportation, even if
individuals brought only their personal effects with them? And
could they be refused the right to take their tools, their machines,
their instruments of work, with them to a land where everything
had to be built? Had anyone accurately calculated the material difficulties involved in such an enterprise? The largest colonization
expedition known to history was that of the Carthaginian Hanno,
who, leaving to found colonies beyond the Pillars of Hercules, led
thirty thousand people carried in sixty ships, each with fifty
rowers.[90] Here it was a matter of a much longer crossing and a
population *twenty* times greater than that transported by Hanno!
Constantine had brought three hundred thousand Sarmatians to
Italy;[91] and in modern times, approximately two hundred thousand Poles were sent to Siberia.[92] But land migrations do not offer

90. Hanno, the Carthaginian mariner, founded various colonies in West Africa
prior to 480 B.C. "Hanno (1)," *The Oxford Classical Dictionary*, ed. N. G. L. Ham-
mond and H. H. Scullard (Oxford, 1970), 487–88.
91. Prior to roughly 250 B.C. the nomadic Sarmatians lived east of the Tanais
River. Over the next three hundred years they slowly migrated westward; eventually large numbers of them were settled within Roman territory by Constantine.
"Sarmatae," *ibid.*, 952; "Sarmatae," *Der kleine Pauly Lexikon der Antike*, ed. Konrat
Ziegler *et al.* (5 vols.; Stuttgart, 1964–75), I, col. 1557.
92. As a result of repeated uprisings, Russia in the nineteenth century sent

the same difficulties to large groups of people as crossing the sea. Moreover, Italy, depopulated in the time of Constantine, had ready resources for the immigrants; and even Siberia is a locality with cities, roads, cultivated farmland, and means to support people.

But what countries were prepared to welcome black deportees from the United States? Where did we want to send these exiles? We would be sending them to the inhospitable land of Africa, where they would die of hunger, like victims set out to die by ancient peoples. If we only wanted to get rid of them, even if it meant sending them to a certain death, why not just throw them straight into the sea? Don't we know that uncultivated land cannot support more than three or four colonists per square league? A dense population would die under such conditions in a few months, even in a few days. How large an area would be needed, therefore, to relocate five million people, in the middle of an uninhabited country, and under conditions where they could survive? But if this area is immense, it would be necessary to penetrate far inland; and then how would provisions be supplied? Before roads could be built, those in the interior of the country would die of hunger. Is the plan rather to send these unfortunate beings to an area that is already inhabited? Tell us which country is going to receive them. Is it France or England, neither of which has vacant land (at least in large amounts) or enough work to provide for this enormous surplus of workers? Is it Asia? Is it South America or Mexico? What country would accept the sudden influx of five million foreigners? What would it do with them? Where would it put them? What effect would this crushing competition

---

thousands of Poles into exile. Some historians estimate that as a consequence of the 1830 insurrection alone 45,000 families were transported to Siberia and the Caucasus. R. F. Leslie, *Polish Politics and the Revolution of November 1830* (London, 1956), 267.

have on its own workers? Yes, indeed, you lack workers in the United States and you talk of sending, at an immense expense, five million of them, five million persons belonging to your working class, to countries that do not want them!

Nor is this all. On what do you base your right to deport these men? Although our ancestors were kidnapped from Africa, we ourselves were born in the United States. Who will deny that we are the children of this country? We were brought up among you, we speak your language, we share your ideas, we partake of your civilization. We fought in your army, our regiments side by side with the regiments of your own soldiers. Your flag is our own— the symbol of our American nationality. We do not want to leave our country; and what right do you have to force us to do so?

These plans for deportation thus agitated public opinion in the South in vain. They have not yet ceased to preoccupy a few minds more filled with hatred than practicality.[93] Organizations exist in favor of the voluntary emigration of blacks; and side by side with these, as if to answer their folly, there are organizations promoting workers' immigration from the Orient. If strong arms are necessary, why should we not use those found at home? This project of mass deportation never took strong root in the country. Our simple protest was enough to counter it.

This was the time, in fact, as I just mentioned, that ideas began to change, especially in the North, concerning the previously enslaved race. Milliken's Bend, Port Hudson, Fort Wagner, and Petersburg had wiped the smiles off the faces of those who had made fun of colored soldiers.[94] The Freedmen's Bureau opened

93. Talk of deportation continued until the end of the nineteenth century. Fredrickson, *Black Image*, 263–67.

94. Negro soldiers fought ably at the battles for Milliken's Bend (June, 1863), Port Hudson (July, 1863), Fort Wagner (July, 1863), and Petersburg (July, 1864). Dudley T. Cornish, *The Sable Arm: Negro Troops in the Union Army, 1861–1865* (New York, 1956), 142–45, 152–56, 275–78.

thousands of schools where black children proved their ability to learn—an aptitude foolishly doubted by the prejudiced.[95] This was also the time when a handful of whites, braver and more far-sighted than the others, began to move into our camp. These first liberals were men who were moved by deep conviction. The schemers, with whom I shall deal later, only joined the cause the day after; I am speaking here of those who were with us the day before. The most remarkable of these was Thomas J. Durant.[96] He was one of New Orleans' leading lawyers. He knew no superior for purity of character and for sincerity of opinions. He was, moreover, a learned man who continued to read even in the prime of life and who consequently continued to gain knowledge and to progress. His convictions were guided by a clear notion of scientific principles and ideas. Strengthened by the public esteem that he had acquired, he could strike more boldly through the barriers of prejudice than any other. At first, he had helped to found a Freedmen's Aid Association;[97] then he organized, with the help of other liberals, the famous association called the Friends of Universal Suffrage,[98] to which all eyes were at that time turned.

95. The Bureau of Refugees, Freedmen, and Abandoned Lands, known commonly as the Freedmen's Bureau, was originally created by Congress in March, 1865, and ceased operation in June, 1872. Its primary purpose was to assist freedmen in their transition from slavery to freedom. At one time the bureau's largest school system was in Louisiana; in early 1866 it boasted 150 schools, 265 teachers, and 19,000 pupils. White, *Freedmen's Bureau*, 8–12, 177.

96. Thomas Jefferson Durant (1817–1882), a white radical from Pennsylvania, is discussed above, 38–39.

97. Organized in February, 1865, the New Orleans Freedmen's Aid Association had as its goal, according to the *Tribune* of May 2, 1865, "to develop the agriculture of the State of Louisiana by means of the Freedmen, to afford them aid, assistance and counsel, by the means of loans of money or of other objects, by means of education and the diffusion of useful information, and by such other means as the needs and requirements of the Freedmen may, in the judgment of the Association, demand." Houzeau was a member of the board of directors of the Association. *Tribune*, April 13, 1865.

98. The Friends of Universal Suffrage party was founded at a meeting over

My Passage at the New Orleans *Tribune*

This association demanded, in the broadest terms, the total assimilation of the proscribed race into the body of the nation. Suffrage was merely the culmination, the crowning achievement, which would reveal that the work of raising this people up was complete, that nothing remained to be accomplished. It was the highest right: he who enjoyed it could be said, all the more, to possess all the other lesser rights; consequently, to demand suffrage for the black and the colored man implied a simultaneous demand for all the civil and political rights guaranteed to other citizens.

The membership of the Friends of Universal Suffrage consisted of whites and men of African descent. They held a public meeting every week. This was the first time that whites had decided to sit publicly and in a regular manner with blacks. Those who dared to do this were discredited immediately and were put on the *Index*[99] by white society. One must do justice to them by saying that all, or almost all, persisted in spite of this in taking part in the work of the society.

At the time, these tasks were of a truly critical nature. Everything remained to be done, and the effort called for pioneers. I shall only deal here with a few of the more important matters. It is needless to say that in this arduous task the Friends of Universal Suffrage and the *Tribune* acted in conjunction.

Nothing can equal the demonstrative power contained in the action of that Greek who, in order to prove the existence of movement, began to walk in front of the crowd. In a like manner we had just demonstrated to the incredulous, by means of student ex-

---

which Thomas J. Durant presided on June 10, 1865. The organization's primary goal was universal suffrage, but more generally it opposed "any discrimination founded upon origin or birth" and advocated that "all be given a fair chance in the world, with the same rights before the law." *Ibid.*, June 16, July 8, 1865.

99. The *Index* is a list of publications suspected of containing erroneous doctrine which the papacy forbids Roman Catholics to read.

aminations, that the black is just as capable of learning as the white. Similarly, it was by making the ballot available to all that the black's ability to vote in an orderly and intelligent manner could be proven and his understanding of the supreme rights established. In a government where most offices are elective, the ballot holds a high place and constitutes an important mechanism. The European reader therefore should not be surprised that so much attention was devoted to this matter.

If the government does not call upon you to vote, the Friends of Universal Suffrage told the blacks, organize a "voluntary election," to which all those who are today barred from voting will be called. It is as though the nonvoters, in the European countries where the vote is still a privilege, organized their own polls, set the day and hour, counted the ballots, and proclaimed their own elected officials. To do so would be a way of showing that they were worthy of the vote and that they knew how to use it. Simply, it had to be understood that those elected should not believe that they had any legal right to participate in the official assemblies of the state. They merely made up a shadow assembly, an assembly composed of men of both races, which would be the representative of the liberal party.

The idea did not lack boldness; and since one should always give credit where it is due, I must not forget to mention that the idea was first suggested by the lawyer Crane,[100] a friend of

100. A white New Orleanian, William R. Crane was a slaveholder before the war. During Reconstruction he served as a delegate from the First Ward to the Friends of Universal Suffrage Convention of September, 1865, chairman of the advisory committee of the New Orleans branch of the Freedmen's Savings and Trust Company, and president of the central executive committee of the Republican party of Louisiana. The *Tribune* referred to Crane as a "veteran of liberalism" and "a friend of our race, who has his whole soul in the cause of universal freedom." *New Orleans Riots*, 173–76; *Tribune*, June 2, 18, 23, September 2, 17, 1865, December 3, 13, 15, 1866, June 2, 1867. The quotations are from the *Tribune*, October 29, 1867, February 9, 1865.

Durant. It was strongly supported by the *Tribune*, and all necessary preparations were made by the Friends of Universal Suffrage.
This movement, which was unique in its own way, was described
at the time through my articles in various newspapers in Paris,
London, and Berlin. The proslavery newspapers appeared to pay
no attention to it; but their party was nonetheless put strongly on
the defensive by it. It was in fact a first sign of life that they gladly
would have stifled. Since the Friends of Universal Suffrage met at
night, and as there were black and colored men among them, it
was decided to revive for this occasion that article of the Code
Noir that forbade blacks to assemble after nine o'clock. At the
stroke of nine, the local police were to enter, break up the meeting, and make a list of those present. Durant and his friends were
to be dragged into court in the midst of blacks and colored men.
"What a humiliation!" said the proslavery men. This great citizen
would have proudly borne such an outrage—not the outrage of
appearing in the company of men whom he respected in spite of
the color of their skin, but that against the right of assembly in a
city of the American Republic.

The military authorities who at that time still governed New
Orleans insisted, however, that the voluntary election was legal
and that no one had the right to oppose it. Voting places were
soon chosen in the eleven wards of the city; committees met to
issue voting certificates to the nonelectors of each district. The
same territorial boundaries used in the official elections were followed, the same day of the week was chosen, the same voting
hours. Finally, on September 11, 1865,[101] men belonging to the
proscribed race went to the polls and cast their ballots. Never had

101. The election was on September 16, 1865. Houzeau was elected as a delegate from the Fourth Ward. He received 2,538 votes. Oscar J. Dunn, the future
lieutenant governor of Louisiana, also received 2,538 votes. *Tribune*, September 19,
1865.

an election been held with such a constant and perfect order. There were no mobs, no singing, no drunken scenes, no tumult. Conditions were such that the next day we were able to say: "Here was an election which the whites would do well to take as an example!"

As for those elected, they were divided equally between Caucasians and Africans. The whites were chosen among citizens already known at this time for their liberalism. The blacks and the mulattoes had elected their most capable and esteemed men to the assembly.[102]

This voluntary election took place on the same day in rural areas, in the midst of various difficulties caused by the ill will of the supporters of slavery. The result was a convention "without distinction between colors" representing the entire state.[103] Durant was elected president by acclamation, and he was the soul of the convention. "We are isolated," he proclaimed;

we began our labors all alone, in the heart of a southern state. It is necessary above all to establish connections, to ally ourselves with the great liberal party of the country— the party which in the United States is called the Republican party. We must henceforth abandon our name of Friends of Universal Suffrage and call ourselves the Repub-

102. On September 10, 1865, the *Tribune* encouraged Negro voters to elect "our most commendable and praiseworthy citizens," and not be "deterred from choosing men of intelligence and wealth, who are not in the habit of mingling with politics."

103. A review of the delegates reveals that only a handful of Louisiana's parishes were represented at the Convention of the Friends of Universal Suffrage, which met in New Orleans from September 25–29, 1865. Privately, even the president of the convention admitted that "it was premature, but no harm was done." *Tribune*, September 26, 29, 1865; Thomas J. Durant to B. F. Butler, October 2, 1865, in Jessie A. Marshall (comp.), *Private and Official Correspondence of Gen. Benjamin F. Butler During the Period of the Civil War* (5 vols.; Norwood, Mass., 1917), V, 669.

licans of Louisiana. We shall inscribe on our flag all the great principles which the northern liberals have determined to defend, and we shall ask the national Republican party to help us to obtain equal rights.[104]

At that time the name Friends of Universal Suffrage was so dear to the men involved in this bitter struggle that all Durant's personal influence was needed to bring about the change, one might even say sacrifice. The *Tribune* submitted, but only with the deepest regret.[105] The course of events, however, revealed that Durant's proposal was truly wise. For by becoming members of the national Republican party, the liberals of Louisiana not only received the support of the members of this entire body, but they were able to bring pressure more easily to bear on this party in order to gain its support for new progressive measures.

The *Tribune*, which had been the "official organ" of the Friends of Universal Suffrage, became "the official organ of the Republican party of Louisiana." This unity between a party and a newspaper added authority to the publication so designated. We ceased to express the opinion, isolated perhaps, of a few individuals. Now we raised our voices in the name of a political organization, still weak among voting citizens, but whose disfranchised supporters numbered millions. From that moment on we had the sympathy and the support of these masses. Our standard became theirs.[106]

104. According to the *Tribune* of September 26, 1865, the free Negro Bernard Soulié first proposed that the convention rename the Friends of Universal Suffrage party the Republican party.

105. On September 26, 1865, the *Tribune* opposed the merger, charging that the Republican party was suspect on the question of universal suffrage and warning that the Friends of Universal Suffrage might become mere "tools" if aligned with the Republicans.

106. *The motto inscribed in large type at the masthead of the* Tribune *was as follows: To Every Citizen His Rights: Universal Suffrage. Equality Before the Law. To Every Laborer His Due: An Equitable Salary and Weekly Payments. Eight Hours a Legal Day's Work.—*

Before adjourning, the convention of the Friends of Universal Suffrage, having become the convention of the Republican party of Louisiana, adopted a petition to Congress in which the purposes of the association were boldly stated. Colonel Warmoth,[107] a young Federal officer who after the war had taken up residence in Louisiana, was charged with taking this petition to Congress.

Existing side by side but independently of the Friends of Universal Suffrage was a liberal party that was sympathetic to the colored race without, however, mixing with it.[108] The more we pushed forward, the more the members of this party realized that five million freed men were not without power. But they limited themselves still to telling them, as they had already done in the colored convention of 1865: "Entrust your interests to our care and let us handle them. We must first wait until the prejudice against you disappears."

How could the colored man heed such advice? How could he hesitate between the Friends of Universal Suffrage, who participated in his assemblies and who told him, "Forward, march, together," and these doctrinaires who had every intention of keeping the upper hand while counseling "patience"? The first group had a noble ambition, that of rising in the world by raising the

HOUZEAU. This motto may be found, for example, in the *Tribune* of December 30, 1866, but there were other mottos over the years. On May 20, 1865, the masthead read: "Practical Results of Secession: The Rebellion Crushed. The Slaves Free."

107. Henry Clay Warmoth (1842–1931), a native of Illinois, settled in New Orleans during the Civil War. A lieutenant colonel in the Union army, Warmoth was appointed judge of the provost court in New Orleans in 1864, and in 1865 he was elected territorial delegate to Congress from Louisiana. He also served as governor of Louisiana from 1868 to 1872. See above, 47, 56, and Francis B. Harris, "Henry Clay Warmoth, Reconstruction Governor of Louisiana," *Louisiana Historical Quarterly*, XXX (1947), 523–654.

108. Houzeau wrote that the well-meaning whites "would like to play the role of protector and always distinguish themselves as whites. They wound in rendering service." Houzeau to Bouvy, May 28, 1867, in Liagre Papers. For a discussion of the moderate Republicans, see McCrary, *Abraham Lincoln*, 211–70; Binning, "Carpetbaggers' Triumph," 21–39.

black men along with them. The second group, faced with a reaction which, under President Andrew Johnson, was growing each day, would willingly have befriended the blacks, but on the condition of remaining their masters. They hoped to use the blacks for support, yet at the same time to avoid sullying themselves through contact with these wretched pariahs. They planned to use them, but not to serve them. Hence how irritated they became when I asked the following question, which struck home: "Why would the black, with equal qualifications, not be as suited to hold public office as you are?"

What could we hope to gain from the support of these men who constantly repeated: "You are moving too fast, asking too much. You are frightening your own friends, scaring them off!" If the blacks had not protested in the name of principle and had not claimed that a free man is the same thing as a citizen, on what ground would they have stood? That of half rights and half measures? This would have meant humiliating themselves and at the same time compromising the future. And if we proclaimed, "The free man is a citizen," could we do otherwise than to demand his rights, all those rights that belong to every citizen?

What, then, should we say of the advice: "First let prejudice disappear, and then you can demand your rights"? What prejudice has ever yielded to discussion alone? In the entire course of history, there is not one that did not have to be overthrown by force. Prejudice is not a matter of reason;[109] it is absurd, then, to expect it to yield to rational argument. Two centuries of effort by mission-

109. In the *Tribune* of May 30, 1865, Houzeau wrote that "those who are waiting for the prejudice of color to disappear before the teachings of education, the sentiments inculcated by Christian religion, and the lights thrown by our advanced civilization, are not conversant with the history of human customs and manners. Should they wait one or two centuries longer, it would still be in vain. Prejudices never die; they have to be killed. . . . the opinion against which we are contending is not founded in reason, and therefore is not reasonable. Legislation alone can bring a remedy to the madness."

aries, newspapers, and men of good sense had remained powerless to prevent widows in Malabar from burning themselves on
their spouses' funeral pyres.[110] Nothing else but a law would have
put an end to this barbarous custom. The overthrow of prejudice
is everywhere a question of authority and not of propaganda. Far
from diminishing from year to year, it is always the nature of
prejudice to become more deeply ingrained. Since prejudice de-
pends upon a preconceived notion, the longer this notion subsists,
the more entrenched and pronounced it becomes. Did the most
horrible of prejudices, that of human sacrifice, which seemed so
easy to combat, ever yield among any people to the effort of persuasion? Everywhere a law was necessary, a severe law, enforced
by inflexible authorities, to rid society of it. In Mexico, it was
Cortés' iron rule that put an end to the sacrifices.[111] In the states
dependent on the Roman Empire, it was Hadrian.[112] At Salamis, it
was Diphilus who, in the sacrifices offered to Aglauros, the
daughter of Cecrops, forced the people to substitute a bull for the
human victim.[113] At Heliopolis, it was Amasis who through his

110. Malabar, a region on the southwest coast of India, suffered for centuries
from *sati*, the practice of self-immolation performed by Hindu women upon the
death of their husbands. The custom was legally abolished by the British in 1829.
Kalikinkar Datta, *Education and Social Amelioration of Women in Pre-Mutiny India*
(Patna, 1963), 63–126; Nigel Davies, *Human Sacrifice in History and Today* (New
York, 1981), 107–26.

111. The practice of human sacrifice survived Cortés' initial proscriptions but
not his destruction of most of Tenochtitlán in 1521 and his campaign to convert
the Aztecs to Christianity. See Davies, *Human Sacrifice*, 198–241; Robert Ricard,
*The Spiritual Conquest of Mexico: An Essay on the Evangelizing Methods of the Mendicant
Orders in New Spain, 1523–1572*, trans. Lesley B. Simpson (1933; Berkeley, 1966).

112. The Roman Emperor Hadrian (A.D. 76–138) took special interest in his
provinces; he eventually abolished the practice of human sacrifice throughout the
empire. *The Cambridge Ancient History*, vol. XI: *The Imperial Peace, A.D. 70–192*, ed.
S. A. Cook, F. E. Adcock, and M. P. Charlesworth (Cambridge, 1954), 439, 445,
646. Houzeau took this and several of his other examples of human sacrifice from
the Greek philosopher Porphyry. See *Porphyry on Abstinence from Animal Food*, ed.
Esme Wynne-Tyson and trans. Thomas Taylor (London, 1965), 104.

113. Wynne-Tyson, *Porphyry*, 102–103. See also the brief discussion of the
shrine to Aglauros at Salamis on the island of Cyprus in "Aglauros," *Paulys Real-*

authority had these victims replaced by effigies.[114] To wait for the prejudice to disappear—what mockery! It is the lawmaker who must take the initiative. It is he who must use an iron hand to batter down these inequities. Only then do opinions and points of view change, only then are habits and customs transformed.

A first example, one not without interest, revealed a little later how well founded were our ideas on the matter. Buses, drawn by mules along rails that followed the main streets, were of two kinds. One kind was reserved exclusively for whites and had no special identifying mark. The other, for people with African blood, was marked for all to see with a large star. Not only was this mark humiliating to the man of color, but it was prejudicial to him because it forced him to wait while three or four buses passed before he could make use of this means of transportation, whereas the white could freely board any of these vehicles. There was nothing in the company's contract that authorized these distinctions; prejudice alone had created them. After freeing the blacks, after extending civil rights to the African race, an extension that I will discuss in a moment, how could one justify the perpetuation of these differences? And yet reasoning, complaints, petitions, sarcasm even, had not made the company yield one iota. Judges ruled, against all principles of law, that a public transport company is free to classify its passengers in order to maintain an orderly service. This means that it could, for example, oblige all those dressed in a certain manner, whom it did not want to carry immediately, to wait for a second train even though they would have paid the same fare as those in the train now leaving. We thus had no hope of winning the battle, either through logic or

Encyclopädie der classischen Altertumswissenschaft, ed. Georg Wissowa *et al.* (34 vols.; Stuttgart, 1894–1972), I, col. 828.

114. Wynne-Tyson, *Porphyry*, 103. The reign of the sixth century B.C. Egyptian Pharaoh Amasis is discussed in Herodotus, *The Histories*, ed. A. R. Burn and trans. Aubrey de Sélincourt (Harmondsworth, 1972), 197–201.

through common sense. But at that time the commanding general (Sheridan) summoned the director of the bus line and told him: "Erase your stars and make all your buses open to all."[115] The next day travel on the city buses had taken on an entirely new aspect. Whites and blacks could be found on each car, and this system seemed so natural that it appeared to have always been in force. Two years of propaganda and public protest had accomplished nothing against a prejudice which by the order of a military commander had fallen in one hour!

Could we find a clearer example? But as time went on, it became evident that prejudice, if left to itself, would survive indefinitely in all relationships between the two races where the authority of the legislator did not intervene. But at that time the national assembly in Washington needed to be encouraged, supported by the population. It realized that it was more advanced than the country as a whole, and it did not dare to go beyond certain limits. It limited itself to a law, to which I referred just a moment ago, that guaranteed all citizens the same *civil rights*.[116] The blacks were freed from their handicaps: henceforth, they could move freely within the Republic; and despite local customs and the opposition of planters, they could make contracts, buy and sell real estate, give testimony, be jurors, and legally marry. This constituted, in a word, equality before civil justice.[117] But Congress hesitated to pronounce equality of political rights.

115. Philip H. Sheridan (1831–1888), commander of the Fifth Military District from March–September, 1867, refused in a meeting with streetcar officials on May 6, 1867, to enforce the star system. That evening the company instructed its drivers "not to make any distinction hence forth between passengers on account of color." *Tribune*, May 7, 1867; Roger A. Fischer, *The Segregation Struggle in Louisiana, 1862–77* (Urbana, 1974), 30–40.

116. The Civil Rights Act, passed on April 9, 1866, over President Andrew Johnson's veto, offered the first federal statutory definition of citizenship and declared the right of the federal government to intervene in state affairs where necessary to protect the rights of United States citizens.

117. *Under the Code Noir, there was no legal marriage for the slave: he could achieve nothing greater than concubinage, and all children were necessarily illegitimate.*—HOUZEAU.

This was not, however, because all unprejudiced men, men of good sense, did not see the necessity of beginning this great reform. Each day experience showed that without the right to vote there was no effective protection for the black. If he appeared before a court, he found judges elected by another caste and belonging to this caste themselves. He would have to be unquestionably innocent to obtain justice. Or if he dealt with a public agency, the spirit of this agency was that of the caste that filled its ranks, directed against the black petitioner. Or if he was dealing with a bureaucrat, the bureaucrat belonged to the white caste and was almost always prejudiced. Nowhere was there an equal balance; oppression was manifest. Its source lay in the partiality that permeated every aspect of local government. It was, therefore, at the root that this essential evil had to be attacked. And it was obvious that in a government where the major offices are elective, any class denied the vote is necessarily sacrificed: it obtains neither equal justice, nor the redress of wrongs, nor even its rightful part of protection in society. For these reasons it was necessary to abolish all distinctions of race where the right to vote was concerned as a general measure in behalf of equality and civilization, quite apart from any political considerations.

On the other hand, a principle contained in the American Declaration of Independence states that there is no legitimate taxation without representation. Even the slave had been represented, al-

---

Actually, the Louisiana Code Noir of 1724 was remarkable for recognizing the marriage state among slaves. Nevertheless, slaves were not allowed to marry without the consent of their masters, and by 1825 the Louisiana Civil Code stated that "their marriages do not produce any of the civil effects which result from such contract[s]." Whatever the law, only a tiny percentage of Louisiana slaves were ever married in legally binding civil or religious ceremonies. Charles Gayarré, *History of Louisiana* (4 vols.; 1866; New Orleans, 1885), I, 531–32; John C. Hurd, *The Law of Freedom and Bondage in the United States* (2 vols.; Boston, 1858), II, 160, where the 1825 Civil Code is quoted; Joe Gray Taylor, *Negro Slavery in Louisiana* (Baton Rouge, 1963), 123; Paul Lachance, "Intermarriage and French Cultural Persistence in Late Spanish and Early American New Orleans," *Histoire sociale-Social History*, XV (1982), 68.

beit fictively. From the beginning, the white population of the South had elected a number of representatives determined by the number of free people with the addition of three-fifths of the slave population. But now that these men were free and that each one counted not for three-fifths of a man but for a whole one, would the whites still cast their votes? Was this in accord with the spirit of the institutions? And if black men were not used to determine the electoral base and did not participate in the election of representatives, could they then logically be taxed? What had happened to this principle in the name of which the nation had proclaimed its independence and which was even its charter, "no taxation without representation"?

Nevertheless, the northern liberal party would have wished to avoid a heated debate in Congress. It would have preferred that the individual states take the initiative, even though this might result in delays and even restrictions in the granting of suffrage. In the summer of 1866, no one expected to see the Congress of the United States take up this question. But if it became a matter of settling these issues in Louisiana alone, how could any other result than an absolute refusal be hoped for? Here, in fact, was a constitutional question, and any convention elected by white voters alone was sure to be dominated by a majority in favor of slavery. There had been, it was true, a liberal convention in 1864, the one that had abolished slavery in the state, including the parishes excepted by Lincoln.[118] But this convention had been elected at a time when the Confederates, not really believing in the seriousness of any of these reforms, had abstained from voting. Today

118. The Louisiana Constitution of 1864, which abolished slavery, incorporated the freedmen's schools into the state educational system, and authorized the state legislature to extend the right to vote to free Negroes on the basis of military service, property holding, and intellectual fitness, was ratified on September 5, 1864. For a detailed account of the constitution and the convention that created it, see McCrary, *Abraham Lincoln*, 237–70.

their political situation was different. They constituted the overwhelming majority of whites; they were regaining local power
through normal electoral channels.

Throughout the South, state legislatures that were boldly
proslavery had just been elected, and the military governors had
been obliged to suspend almost all the laws they had enacted. The
Louisiana State Legislature, in particular, had established a cate-
gory of "apprenticeship" that was merely a new form of slavery,
reinstated corporal punishment, bound the blacks to the soil, and
passed an iniquitous "vagrant" law that would have permitted the
seizing and renting out to planters of any colored man on the
street, whoever he might be. At the same time, education was refused to blacks. The whole thing was odious; and as a reaction it
was absurd, for it was too early and too bold an action. This error,
like many others, helped our cause. Each day the northern newspapers borrowed and reprinted directly from the *Tribune* the text
of this new Code Noir and our comments on it. The whole country protested against it. The government could not permit anyone
to demolish its work in this way and to defy it the day after the fall
of Richmond. The military commanders used their power to suspend all this ridiculous legislation.[119] The Freedmen's Bureau gave
the blacks more effective protection, the need for which was evident.[120] It responded to reactionary provocations by multiplying
the number of schools. But, as we can see, there was nothing to be
gained from these blind men whose passions endangered their
most cherished interests.

119. The Louisiana Black Codes, which actually did not go quite so far toward
restoring slavery as did the codes of other southern states, were enacted by a special session of the state legislature in the fall of 1865. These codes aroused northern opinion and spurred passage of the Civil Rights Act of 1866. Joe Gray Taylor,
Louisiana Reconstructed, 1863–1877 (Baton Rouge, 1974), 99–103.

120. The *Tribune* was rarely satisfied with the protection offered by the bureau.
See, for example, the issues of August 31, December 14, 1865, February 2, May 11,
August 12, 1866.

Someone noticed that the Convention of 1864 had not been dissolved: it had been indefinitely adjourned, "authorizing its president to re-assemble it." Let the convention reassemble then, and in its liberal spirit vote in favor of universal suffrage. This plan was developed in the *Tribune* in February, 1866. But we could not throw ourselves totally behind it.[121] First of all, there were various specific obstacles of which I shall speak later; and besides, the legitimacy of this new action after two years of silence would always be contested. But above all we wanted to force Congress to settle the question. A general ruling, invariable and liberal, was preferable to the uncertain and diverse actions of state assemblies, actions which, moreover, could be reversed at the first change of a majority. Also, it was a matter of general, not state interest, and good logic dictated that it should be a federal law and not a variety of state laws that would set the basis for the right to vote.

The *Tribune* therefore took a waiting stance. It could not oppose the attempt to establish universal suffrage in Louisiana; it always expressed sympathy and support for the authors of this proposal, but it did not approve of the means suggested.

The president of the convention, the Federal Judge Durell,[122] refused to take the responsibility of reconvening this assembly. "The result of the debate," he stated,

> was that this eventual convention should only be held if the Constitution of 1864 had been rejected by the vote of the

121. When asked in December, 1866, whether the *Tribune* had advocated the "doctrines" of those who sought to reconvene the Constitutional Convention of 1864, Houzeau responded: "It only advocated the assembling of the convention for the purpose of testing judicially whether it was a legal body or not." *New Orleans Riots*, 76.

122. Edward H. Durell (1810–1887), a native of Portsmouth, New Hampshire, and graduate of Harvard College, had moved to New Orleans in 1837. He was mayor of New Orleans by military appointment in 1863 and judge of the federal district court in New Orleans from 1863–1874. *New Orleans Riots*, 260–63; Allen Johnson and Dumas Malone (eds.), *Dictionary of American Biography* (20 vols.; New York, 1928–36), V, 545–46.

people. In this case, I would have recalled the assembly, in order to begin our labors anew. But after the people had approved what we had done, to recall the assembly would be in violation of the spirit of the resolution and would give our mandate an extension which violates the principles of popular government if we were to perpetuate ourselves in power and were to settle questions of which our constituents were not even aware when they elected us. A new convention elected directly from the people is needed; I will not sign to recall the [old] convention.[123]

This answer was dictated, it cannot be denied, by a true feeling for the essential meaning of democracy. Several precedents were cited against it, that of Missouri, for example, where a constitutional convention was reconvened three different times and lasted four years.[124] But Durell was unmovable.

Nothing could be accomplished without him. In May, 1866, however, he took a three-month vacation and left for the North.[125] Who, then, in his absence was president of the former convention? Did not the absence of the president authorize a majority of its members to name a temporary president to replace the absent one? And furthermore, whatever the authority that brought about the convocation, once a majority of the convention met and declared themselves duly reconvened, were not their former powers as members reestablished and everything become normal again?

123. Durell had doubts about the legality of reconvening the Constitutional Convention of 1864, but evidently his primary reason for refusing to reconvene the convention was his belief that it "could not be assembled without a riot." *New Orleans Riots*, 262.

124. The Missouri convention to which Houzeau is referring first met in early 1861 to consider the question of secession. Prior to adjourning, it established a committee that if necessary could reconvene the convention. The convention met five times between February, 1861, and June, 1863. William E. Parrish, *Turbulent Partnership: Missouri and the Union, 1861–1865* (Columbia, 1963), 7–141.

125. Durell left New Orleans for New York on July 7 and did not return until November 15, 1866. *New Orleans Riots*, 261.

This was how certain members of the convention reasoned. Although these did not yet form a majority, they undertook the responsibility to elect, in a rather officious meeting, a provisional president—Judge Howell of the Louisiana Court of Appeals.[126] He convoked the assembly, and the civil governor of the state, Mr. Wells, endorsed it and set the date for by-elections for the few vacant seats.[127]

The *Tribune* was first to publish these official notifications. It was a sensational stroke. The proslavery forces now could not ignore that the convention would meet with sufficient numbers, that it would declare itself duly assembled, and that within twenty-four to forty hours, it would have declared universal suffrage, called for new elections, and established and authorized the election of new assemblies that would be the product of a vote in which blacks would participate. This would mean the total and absolute overthrow of the proslavery faction. It would have been a great revolution, which would have traveled from Louisiana through all the other southern states. In a word, this would have been the planters' Waterloo, and they had to prevent it.

How they acted to suppress this legal, or quasi-legal, move-

126. Rufus K. Howell was an associate justice of the Louisiana Supreme Court when elected president *pro tem* at a preliminary meeting of the members of the 1864 constitutional convention in New Orleans on June 26, 1866. A member of the city school board and a district court judge before the war, Howell had by late 1866 concluded that "the first essential step" to reconstructing Louisiana was "to break the local power of the secession element. In other words, to take the local control out of the present hands, and hold the State until the people themselves have developed a sufficient attachment to the government of the United States to do justice to all the inhabitants of the State, irrespective of color or origin." *Ibid.*, 50–51.

127. J. Madison Wells (1808–1899), governor of Louisiana, 1865–1867, was the only native Louisianian to serve as governor of the state during Reconstruction. Wells's decision to assist the radicals in reconvening the convention of 1864 came as something of a surprise, for only a few months before he had opposed the idea of Negro suffrage. Walter M. Lowrey, "The Political Career of James Madison Wells," *Louisiana Historical Quarterly*, XXXI (1948), 995–1123.

ment I will describe later, and those who knew the planters, I admit, should have guessed what would happen. For the moment, the initiators of this measure were lulled by a pure and simple discussion of the legality of the projected meeting. Those who planned to participate in the convention were threatened with arrest, imprisonment, and trial. It is true that the proslavery legislature, elected after the reestablishment of peace under the old law of white suffrage, was not in session. But the city council and the mayor of New Orleans, elected by the same suffrage, were devoted body and soul to their own reelection. The police force of this great city, under their control, was composed not only of hotheaded whites, but almost entirely of ex-Confederate soldiers who had returned home.[128] Nothing would have been easier than to have the members of the convention arrested and then get them convicted by judges elected by the same limited suffrage.

The first meeting was scheduled for Monday, July 30, 1866, at noon. The assembly was held in the legislative hall on the second floor of the statehouse.[129] I was present, sitting in the reserved section;[130] and although there was some commotion outside and a certain number of blacks who out of curiosity had gathered around the meeting place, nothing gave a hint of the violent scenes that were to occur shortly. The enemy had concealed his attack columns until the last moment.

An attempt was made in the ensuing carnage to snuff out the effort to give men of the African race political rights. By turning the issue into a bloodbath, the planters imagined that it could never again be brought to the fore and that they would have won.

At about one o'clock in the afternoon during a recess in the

128. On the Confederate invasion of the New Orleans police force, see *New Orleans Riots*, 4, 67, 95, 238.

129. *Most commonly known by the name Mechanics' Institute.*—HOUZEAU.

130. Houzeau attended the convention in his capacity as editor of the *Tribune*. *New Orleans Riots*, 73.

meeting, the city hall bell, the bell of this new St. Bartholomew,[131] sounded the same signal that at the time of the Confederacy had announced the approach of the Federal fleet. At that sound, squads of policemen armed with revolvers, companies of voluntary firemen also armed with pistols and axes, and auxiliaries organized from secret proslavery societies, set off from different points in the city. At the head of one of these groups marched a southern officer who for this great occasion had put on his Confederate uniform and sword.[132]

The outcome of such a battle between two groups, the one highly organized with leaders, arms, a plan, and the other a mass of curious and inoffensive men without arms, without leaders or tactics, this outcome, we must admit, was never in doubt. It was not a battle, but a frightful massacre.[133] The crowd of blacks who

131. On August 23, 1572, the bells of St. Germain l'Auxerrois, the church across from the royal palace in Paris, rang in the feast of St. Bartholomew and the massacre of all Protestants in the city. Many Protestants were in Paris to celebrate the wedding of their leader, Henry of Navarre, and Charles IX's sister, Margaret of Valois. See N. M. Sutherland, *The Massacre of St. Bartholomew and the European Conflict, 1559–1572* (London, 1973). Houzeau drew the same analogy in the *Tribune* on September 11, 1866, where he explicitly compared Andrew Johnson's role in the New Orleans Riot to that of Charles IX in the St. Bartholomew Day Massacre. Houzeau also alludes to the St. Bartholomew Day Massacre in a letter describing the riot to his brother. Saying that he had never seen "such cold-blooded horrors," Houzeau attributed the riot to the "effect of a long possession of man by man. The moral sense is destroyed, in every respect. These men do not see themselves committing a crime. For them this is a little preventive antidote against the reformers and the anarchists." Houzeau to his brother Auguste, August 5, 1866, in Houzeau Papers. This letter is reproduced in its entirety in the Appendix.

132. *The truth was established in the official report of General Baird.*—HOUZEAU. Baird's report does not mention the southern officer in Confederate garb, but it is otherwise in agreement with Houzeau's description. The riot, according to Baird, presented "a picture of atrocity having no parallel in American history." *New Orleans Riots*, 461–62.

133. On August 2, 1866, Philip H. Sheridan, then commanding general of the Department of the Gulf, advised General U. S. Grant: "The more information I obtain of the affair of the 30th in this city, the more revolting it becomes. It was no riot. It was an absolute massacre by the police, which was not excelled in murderous cruelty by that of Fort Pillow. It was a murder which the mayor and police of the city perpetrated without the shadow of a necessity." *New Orleans Riots*, 351.

milled around the assembly hall was attacked without warning. Assaulted from both ends of the street, retreat was impossible, and all they could do was divide themselves into two groups to face each of the aggressors. But they had only their fists and a few stones. Under continuous fire, this group slowly withdrew to the statehouse portico.

At the first firing of revolvers, a member of the convention, Dr. Hire, a Scotsman by birth and a long-standing abolitionist, called me to his side to show me the first of the wounded brought up to the second floor.[134] He wanted me to take down his name and deposition. While we were speaking, the windows of the assembly hall, shattered by bullets, began to fly in all directions, and we were showered by splinters of glass.

The *Tribune* was without any responsibility in this matter; we did not even have to reproach ourselves for imprudence, as we had neither endorsed this convention nor encouraged people to attend. I would have wished, nevertheless, to establish, or would have wished to see the promoters of the convention establish, some means to protect and defend it. I went to several black friends whom I noticed in the auditorium and asked whether they were armed. All told me that they had not expected any attack and that they had no arms. In fact, foreseeing the rumored arrests, most had avoided bringing knives and revolvers. Resistance was therefore physically impossible. I returned to Howell, who had remained on the podium, and informed him that most members were without arms. I learned at the same time that the members of the convention had no plans. I was still speaking to the president of the assembly when Mr. Gibbons, a reporter for the *Crescent*

134. William Henry Hire, a physician and onetime coroner of New Orleans, relates the same story in *New Orleans Riots*, 64, 66. Shortly after the riot, Houzeau referred to Hire, who had lived in New Orleans since 1845, as "one of my good friends, a doctor of Scottish origin who is now in bed with a dagger wound in the side and a bullet in the head." Houzeau to his brother Auguste, August 5, 1866, in Houzeau Papers.

(an ultra proslavery newspaper),[135] who was associated with Mr. Howell in a secret society, arrived. "I entreat you," he told him, "to think of your life, for I know what has been decided and that the police in particular are authorized to shoot everyone." The president escaped down the service stairs, but after realizing that it was too dangerous to go into the street, he hid in a first-floor office which through good fortune was not searched.[136]

From the front door I watched for a moment this odious massacre, a sort of ambush into which unarmed victims continually fell. Those wounded who still had some strength dragged themselves under the columns whose drenched tiles had become a large pool of blood. I shall always remember a Negro of Herculean size who was still able to stand erect. His face and hands were covered with blood, and he was still holding an enormous stone that he had grabbed apparently in order to defend himself. The expression of indignation that appeared on his face was frightening, and no artist could have reproduced it. I asked him one or two questions, but he heard nothing but the gunshots that were destroying his innocent and defenseless people.

Going into a courtyard of the building, I heard a voice call me and saw one of my friends, who had removed a board from a solid wood fence and was going through the hole to another property behind the attacked building. I, along with five or six other people, followed this friend to the rear of a store that faced on another street. For a moment I thought I was safe. But we were not the only ones to follow this route. Seeing twenty people arrive and knowing that others would probably follow, I had no doubt that we would soon be discovered or followed. That, in

135. Israel Gibbons was a reporter for the *Crescent*, one of the most rabidly conservative papers in New Orleans during Reconstruction. *Mygatt & Co.'s Directory* (New Orleans, 1857), 112. I have silently corrected Houzeau's spelling of Gibbons and a few other surnames.

136. Howell hid in Governor J. Madison Wells's office from one until four o'clock. Upon leaving, he was arrested and jailed. *New Orleans Riots*, 48.

effect, is what happened, and most of those who remained in this place lost their lives there.

I stepped out and walked alone into the street. A few curious blacks who had withdrawn to this parallel artery were also under fire from the conspirators, who were shooting from the two opposite ends of the street. Nevertheless, the attack in this place was less furious. I walked slowly, fearful of attracting the attention of the enemy. A merchant who had closed his shutters on the other side of the street and was returning inside his store to lock himself in noticed me. He was a colored man who knew me. He had the generosity to call me over with his hand—I say generosity, for if I had been recognized or followed, he would have brought the Confederate vengeance down upon himself, and God alone knows whether this vengeance forgives.[137] A wounded black man, whose clothes were bloodstained along one entire side, lay face down almost in front of the door. The hole that the bullet had made in his side could be seen.

The massacre lasted until after three o'clock. The room where the convention had met and where many men had remained was broken into behind blazing weapons. There the Protestant minister, Horton, was shot down as he waved a white flag; Captain Loup was slashed to ribbons by hunting knives; Dr. Dostie was mortally wounded, then dragged through the gutters, and finally thrown on a trash heap, around which the assassins danced and shouted hurrahs for Jefferson Davis. More than one hundred and thirty people lost their lives—all, of course, belonged to the unarmed crowd: not one single person died on the other side.[138] It

137. Houzeau recounts this story in a letter to his brother Auguste on August 5, 1866, in Houzeau Papers.

138. Rev. J. W. Horton, who had delivered the opening prayer at the convention and was later buried with much fanfare in Boston, Captain Constant Loup, who had apparently served in the Union army during the war, and Dr. Anthony P. Dostie, a New York-born dentist who had long been a fiery advocate of Negro suffrage, were among the thirty-eight people officially listed as killed during the

was a scene both cowardly and cruel. Finally, between three and four o'clock the army, whose barracks were in the suburbs, arrived at this scene of slaughter; and from the mayor and his police to the Confederate officer who that day had put on his uniform and returned to active duty, all disappeared as though by magic.

The night was spent removing the bodies and transporting the wounded. But the troops were few and could not guard more than a few points; the colored population and its white friends still lived, alas, under the threat of an all too natural terror.

In the course of these events, I can report with pride that the *Tribune* in no way failed in its duty. During the several weeks of this feverish agitation, we believed each day that the printing plant would be attacked. But the personnel stood up to the storm; it yielded neither to discouragement nor to threats. The newspaper never failed to appear each day and to bear its banner proudly.[139] What filled its pages can be guessed easily enough: first, an energetic protest against the use of violence; then an account of the events, the various episodes of the massacre, the details concerning the deaths of the principal victims, the voluntary accounts of witnesses who came forward to tell of the attackers' odious acts of cowardice and barbarism. It was necessary to enlighten our friends in other states about the true character of this day. It was necessary to arouse the moral sense of the country. All the other newspapers of the city—all white and proslavery—carefully hid the details. They limited themselves to repeating in

---

riot. Only one of the thirty-eight was recorded as an anticonventionist, and he had been accidentally shot by a policeman. One hundred forty-six were recorded as wounded. *Tribune*, September 9, 1866 (French ed.); *New Orleans Riots*, 41, 55, 103, 182, 185, 186, 205, 321, 265.

139. Houzeau stated on December 24, 1866, that the *Tribune* was issued "regularly, except under certain circumstances; for instance, during the days of the riot the editors and compositors did not dare come into the office." *New Orleans Riots*, 76.

unison: "It can be seen from the censure that this attempt brought from our citizens that black suffrage is unthinkable. As for the assembly, it was illegal: the evil with which it menaced us was a clear provocation. We dissolved it, and it was well done." At the same time, the assassins were not searched out. Terror continued to weigh on the city. Isolated killings or at least attempted killings, in lonely streets, were reported every day. It was clear that the weak Federal garrison could not withstand a concerted attack by the Confederate elements. Many white liberals whose lives were openly threatened left the city.[140] At this time in Louisiana, the conqueror was at the mercy of the conquered.

There was a sudden and profound furor in the country. The *Tribune*'s articles were reprinted in the major newspapers in the North. The effect of these events was devastating to the proslavery forces. Not since the assassination of Lincoln, which was another act emanating from the same politics, had the nation felt such indignation.[141] Before a week had passed, the Confederates were able to measure the extent of their mistake. Instead of seeing the plan to extend political rights to the African race drowned in blood, they had on the contrary assured the success of this mea-

---

140. The most prominent radical to leave New Orleans was Thomas J. Durant, who during the riot quietly slipped into a carriage drawn up in the alley behind his office, made his way to the Carrollton levee, and fled north on a Mississippi steamer. Durant eventually arrived in Washington, D.C., where he testified that "a territorial government should be established in Louisiana—I should rather say a quasi-territorial government, supported by military force, and that it should be based on equal suffrage of all citizens without distinction of color; that it should be held in that subjection until it was clear that the citizens of the State were fit to carry on a State government, when they should be permitted to do so, and not until then, however long it might take." Durant never returned to New Orleans. *Ibid.*, 9, 11.

141. Houzeau wrote to his brother Auguste on August 5, 1866, that "the effect [of the Riot] in the North is immense; it will probably be almost as great as that of Lincoln's assassination." In Houzeau Papers. On the North's angry response, see Howard K. Beale, *The Critical Year: A Study of Andrew Johnson and Reconstruction* (1930; New York, 1958), 350–75.

sure and had brought the question before Congress. Here it was agreed on the one hand that the southern liberals, who are but a handful among the white population, must be protected, and on the other hand that the electoral body must be made up of more than an oppressive minority of the population.

When Congress met, it ordered an inquiry, and the members of this congressional commission came to New Orleans.[142] Mr. Laizer and I had private discussions with them. Mr. Laizer, whose premature death we still regret to this day, was connected with the English-language staff of the *Tribune*; he carried out an ungrateful task with a devotion that hastened his end. The son of a Swiss immigrant and a Creole with an infinitesimal amount of African blood in his veins, he was to all appearances white, so much so in fact that he had been admitted without the least suspicion into the printing plants of the Americans. But when the *Tribune* was established, he had declared his hereditary connections with the proscribed race and had taken up the pen to defend his rights. He expressed himself well, easily gained the attention of his readers, and often succeeded in convincing the American readers.[143]

The congressional commission of inquiry consisted of three members. Mr. Eliot of Massachusetts, its chairman, maintained a certain reserve, but it was clear that he recognized the necessities of the situation.[144] Judge Shellabarger from Ohio, who has since become the Minister of the United States in Lisbon, was much more explicit.[145] He brushed aside local prejudices, and, embrac-

142. The House of Representatives passed a resolution creating the Select Committee on the New Orleans Riots on December 6, 1866. *New Orleans Riots*, 62.

143. J. Clovis Laizer, who lived at 256 Robertson Street in 1868, was Houzeau's first staff appointment to the English edition of the *Tribune*. See above, 29; Houzeau to his parents, May 22, 1869, in Houzeau Papers; *Gardner's New Orleans Directory for 1868* . . . (New Orleans, 1868), 256.

144. Thomas D. Eliot (1808–1870) was a Republican representative from Massachusetts from 1859–1869. He had previously served as a Whig from 1854–1855. *Biographical Directory*, 905.

145. Samuel Shellabarger (1817–1896) was a Republican representative from

ing a few great principles—liberal principles—he was willing to accept all the consequences. As for the third member of the commision, Mr. Boyer of Pennsylvania, a representative of the minority, he claimed in his conversations with us to be seeking only the truth and to have come without any preconceived notions.[146] But there was no act of the proslavery forces that he did not find a way to excuse even if it was hostile to the Union or to extenuate even if it was criminal. We did not succeed in making him admit that even acts like assassinations, if committed in the interest of the South, should be condemned.

When they returned to Washington, Mr. Eliot and Mr. Shellabarger because of their leadership positions were the first members of Congress to present bills to deal with the situation in the South. Their two bills embodied the principle of the political equality of all citizens without distinction of color or race. The ensuing debate, however, did not chiefly concern itself with these first proposals, but the Committee on Reconstruction, established to formulate a general law, drew upon all their important points.[147]

Ohio from 1861–1863, 1865–1869, and 1871–1873. He was United States Minister to Portugal in 1869. *Ibid.*, 1686.

146. Benjamin M. Boyer (1823–1887) was a Democratic representative from Pennsylvania from 1865–1869. During the committee's investigation of the riot, Houzeau informed Boyer that the animosity white Louisianians had for Unionists was "only a sequel to their rebellion." In his minority report Boyer held, however, that the riot was "in no wise the result of any hostility or disaffection on the part of the community of New Orleans towards the federal government. It was not in any just or fair sense of the term a vestige or outcrop of the rebellion." *Ibid.*, 623; *New Orleans Riots*, 60, 75.

147. For a discussion of Eliot's bill of early 1867 proposing to replace the existing Louisiana government with a new one that would enfranchise Negroes and disfranchise most whites, see David Donald, *Charles Sumner and the Rights of Man* (New York, 1970), 285–86. For a discussion of Shellabarger's role in the creation of the Reconstruction Act of March 2, 1867, see Eric L. McKitrick, *Andrew Johnson and Reconstruction* (Chicago, 1960), 482–83. Created on December 4, 1865, the Joint Committee on Reconstruction was instructed to inquire into the condition of the states formerly known as the Confederate States of America and to report whether those states were entitled to representation in Congress. All proposed legislation relating to Reconstruction was referred to the committee. *Ibid.*, 258–59.

Hence these were in reality the seeds out of which grew the famous "Reconstruction Acts" that made white and black one single political class.[148]

According to these laws, in all the southern states all citizens were to be registered in an electoral list that would contain the names of black and colored men as well as those of whites.[149] Once these lists had been completed, preparations for the election of a convention would be made in each state; this convention would then draft a state constitution laying the foundations of a new government. If following this, the new government was approved by both houses of Congress, the state would be recognized as a member of the Union, its representatives would return to Congress, from which they had voluntarily removed themselves by "Secession," and the period of revolution would be over.

General Sheridan was the commander of the military district of Louisiana at that time; it was his duty to implement this law in the state. First, he had to name commissioners to prepare the electoral lists. He had to assign three commissioners to each parish, so he had to appoint one hundred fifty persons in all.[150] It seemed natural, at a time when all distinction of color was to disappear from the electoral lists to be prepared, that the commissioners should also be chosen without distinction of race. Blacks had as much right and as much interest as whites in being represented in

148. Between March 2, 1867, and March 11, 1868, Congress passed four Reconstruction acts which divided the South into five military districts, each under the command of a general from the U.S. Army, and specified the conditions, including ratification of the Fourteenth Amendment and formation of a constitution providing for Negro suffrage, under which Congress might readmit southern states. For a discussion of these acts and Shellabarger's influential theory of Reconstruction, see *ibid.*, 113–15, 473–85.

149. The Reconstruction Act of March 2, 1867, disfranchised some disloyal southern whites. *Ibid.*, 482, 484n.

150. Sheridan appointed 141 civilian registrars, three each for forty-seven parishes, and 10 army officers to serve as supervisors-at-large. *Tribune*, April 16, 21, 1867; Dawson, *Army Generals*, 49.

these commissions to ensure that no bias occurred to the detriment of their race. But such was the force of habit, such was the tenacity of prejudice, even among enlightened people, that the general selected all of his commissioners, without exception, from among the white race.[151] It was a bad start, not only because it preserved the old spirit of prejudice at the very moment when it was necessary to act according to the new spirit, but it also threatened to touch off a reaction like that in Saint Domingue, where the ostracism of blacks led through reprisals to the ostracism of whites.[152] Instead of promoting the union of the races, it led the black man to say: "Tomorrow I shall have power through the vote, and I shall do as you have done." This act was more than ill conceived; it was dangerous. I did not hesitate to say this, and I was supported by the northern liberal press.

Not until electoral lists were prepared were the southern white masses convinced that the black man would at last enjoy political rights. Not only the proslavery forces, but men without any defined opinion, the vacillators, had up to now seen our efforts as so much smoke dissipating in the wind. Failing to take account of the changed situation, the southern whites, lulled by routine, had not even glimpsed the necessary chain of events that would force the country to recognize that the freedmen were men like all others. Until the last moment, only incredulity surrounded us. Scarcely

151. Dismayed that Sheridan had not appointed a single Negro registrar, the *Tribune* denounced "those who promise a great deal and always find it is 'too soon' to act," and declared "that the day when equal eligibility to office will be a truth has not come yet, and is not likely to come from any quarter, but from our own votes, when we elect men of our own race." *Tribune*, April 11, 16, 1867. Sheridan subsequently agreed to choose one-third of the registrars from the Afro-American population. *Ibid.*, July 27, 31, 1867.

152. The brutal treatment of Afro-American slaves in Saint Domingue resulted in the execution and deportation of thousands of whites during and after the Haitian Revolution (1791–1804). See James G. Leyburn, *The Haitian People* (New Haven, 1966), chs. 2–3.

two or three ambitious politicians took account of the change, and in order to prepare themselves for any eventuality, convinced themselves that it was good to have connections with both camps. But as soon as the sun rose on a new day, as soon as the "new electors," who almost everywhere formed the majority, became the prospective dispensers of public offices and favors, I saw men who had condemned them the night before, whose hands were stained with the blood of our people, and who today claimed that they had always had the best interests of the black man in their hearts, come running to the *Tribune*, hat in hand, in the attitude of a supplicant.

Finally, the prejudiced liberals who had endlessly told us to count on them but to wait, to go slowly, to allow time to dissipate fears—they also understood that they had been passed over and rendered redundant. The man of color no longer had any need for them; but in order for them to hold public office, they would henceforth need the black and the man of color. After three years of inactivity and silence, during this violent reaction that they had not found the means to combat, they had finally in the eleventh hour founded a newspaper to help them in their egotistic goal— to lift themselves up on the backs of blacks. They called this newspaper the *Republican*. It was a buttress for us when it pleaded in favor of egalitarian principles, but it was an opponent to be fought when it yielded to old prejudices.[153] Between those who had identified themselves with the proscribed race and the Pharisees who insisted on deference in public places and who wanted the best seats reserved at banquets and in synagogues, there could be no true sympathy. The *Republican* was jealous of our influence

153. On April 11, 1867, the day after the *Republican* first appeared, the *Tribune* expressed its hope that the new paper, "though coming late will not be behind in its liberalism" and will "understand well that we want to remodel anew the institutions of the State." A month later the *Tribune* declared the *Republican* "full of prejudice against the colored man." *Tribune*, May 4, 1867.

and embarrassed by our rectitude. This newspaper felt that because it was white and somewhat liberal, all blacks should bow before it and call it "master." Was it possible for the African population to surrender in this way while it was still being led forward by its former defenders, its friends of yesterday, who had been fighting in the breach for four years, and who had always flown its banner?

At the *Tribune* we acted in unison with the old phalanx of the Friends of Universal Suffrage, now called the "Republican Committee."[154] Congress was preparing to designate two newspapers to publish the authentic texts of laws, administrative announcements, and judicial decisions in each southern state. These papers would be designated "official newspapers of the United States." These local publications, which were available to the various groups of the population, took the place of the *Bulletin des lois*, which does not exist in America.[155] Such a designation is vigorously sought after: it sets apart those newspapers thus singled out; it increases their circulation and influence; and the publication of legal and administrative notices is very lucrative. There was a very lively struggle in Washington for the two Louisiana nominations. The reactionary newspapers did not have a chance in this struggle. Among the liberal newspapers, there was the recently founded *Republican* and a country sheet called the *Iliad*, published in the town of Homer by Jasper Blackburn.[156] These

154. Houzeau is referring to the Central Executive Committee of the Republican Party of Louisiana, which was initially dominated by men who were loyal to the *Tribune*. The *Tribune* lost control of the executive committee to forces that were sympathetic to the *Republican* at the party's June, 1867, convention. The struggle for control of the executive committee can be traced in the *Tribune*, April–July, 1867, and in Binning, "Carpetbaggers' Triumph," 21–27.

155. Since the Convention, the official publication of French public acts has been in the *Bulletin des lois*.

156. William Jasper Blackburn (1820–1899), a native of Arkansas, moved to Louisiana in 1849 and founded the *Iliad* in 1859. He was a member of the U.S. House of Representatives, 1868–1869, and of the Louisiana state senate, 1874–

were both white. Then there was the *Tribune*, the pioneer of 1862,[157] which had been published since the first dangerous days, and which had the honor to participate in the entire drama and demand one after the other all the reforms. Here was no ordinary soldier; here was a veteran surrounded by mere draftees.

But whenever mention of this "black newspaper" was made in Congress, a mighty clamor arose. Prejudice reared its ugly head to belittle us. Both white newspapers, each in its own interest, fought to have us excluded. While their editors were in Washington, we witnessed their intrigues from a distance with the attitude of worthy men who have done their duty and who do not lower themselves to intrigue. I limited myself to recalling past services. With such credentials as we have, I said, if we are rejected, it will only be because we are black. Is this the first signal that Congress will give the country the day after proclaiming the equality of rights, and in its first opportunity to demonstrate the value of this new idea? Is equality a reality, then, or is it still only a farce and a lie?

The progressive members of Congress did not want to fail the principles that they had just established. "Select whatever other newspaper you want," said General Butler, "provided that you give me my black newspaper."[158] The role of the *Tribune* was, in effect, so exceptional that the denial of justice would have been so flagrant and the concession to prejudice so clear and so serious that we received the designation. After long discussion, Congress voted an amendment to the law augmenting the number of official

---

1878. As a delegate to the Louisiana Constitutional Convention of 1867–1868, Blackburn opposed the desegregation of public schools and the extension of printing contracts to the *Tribune*. *Biographical Directory*, 598; *Republican*, November 28, 1867, March 1, 1868; Fischer, *Segregation Struggle*, 49, 51–52, 62.

157. Houzeau is suggesting here that the *Tribune*, which began publication in 1864, was simply a continuation of *L'Union*, which did begin publication in 1862.

158. I have been unable to find the quotation attributed to Benjamin F. Butler in the *Congressional Globe*. Butler is identified above, p. 74n.

newspapers in Louisiana to three. Thus the two white newspapers were satisfied, and the audacity of having chosen a colored newspaper was, so to speak, excused.[159]

The position we had just conquered at sword point constituted nonetheless a moral triumph with immense significance. The United States had added a great principle to its fundamental law: "All Americans are equal before the law." And today, the *Tribune*, "founded, edited, [and] printed by men of color," took its place among the official newspapers of this country. Thus the principle of equality received its consecration. It was now true that skin color was no longer grounds for exclusion or preference. It was now true that blacks could claim, when they had the necessary qualifications, the same rights, the same honors, the same rewards as whites. Our success was, in essence, that of the entire race. The triumph of an individual in an election or in any undertaking would not have had the same meaning. The *Tribune* was a collective body, a representative. On the day when it took its place among the official organs of the nation, every black man throughout the Republic realized that the barriers between the two races were forever sundered.

Fusion between races would not result immediately. Nor would homogeneity be established in a day. But the impetus had been given. The forward movement had begun, and who could stop it now?

The election of the state [constitutional] convention that I have already mentioned was held under these circumstances. The supporters of slavery, realizing that blacks would vote as a group for the Republican candidates and that almost everywhere they would receive the majority of the vote, became momentarily very dis-

159. Edward McPherson, clerk of the House of Representatives, notified the *Tribune* of its designation as an official government paper in a letter dated April 11, 1867. *Tribune*, April 17, 1867.

couraged. In many parishes they nominated no candidates and lost the election by default; the "new voters" acted with unity and intelligence. Time was too short for the schemers to hide their true colors and to capture votes. Proven men, known for a long time to the African race, were elected. The elections of September 27 and 28, 1867, were held in an orderly manner and established a convention consisting of one hundred members, of whom the great majority were radicals and who were almost equally divided between the two colors.[160]

Here was the first official assembly in the United States where black men participated with whites.[161] This spectacle was shocking to the supporters of slavery; most of their newspapers pretended not to know about the meeting, as if everything accomplished there had no value.

Later the reactionaries were to beg seats in these assemblies from their former slaves, but in 1867 many of them still naïvely believed that these sweeping reforms were neither serious nor permanent. "We are being tested today," they said; "it is a time of crisis; but tomorrow everything will return to the old order. The

160. At the election of September 27–28, 1867, Louisiana voters overwhelmingly approved the calling of a state constitutional convention, which subsequently met in New Orleans from November 23, 1867, through March 9, 1868, and simultaneously elected to the convention ninety-eight delegates, half of whom were Negroes. Houzeau wrote to his mother that "the greater part of the men of color [at the convention] are very inexperienced. The convention is composed of 98 members, with 9 pure blacks, 40 mulattoes of diverse colors, but light for the most part; and 49 whites. . . . There are not more than 7 whites with us among the 49 at the convention; and there are some mulattoes who have been elected as conservatives and allies of the whites." Houzeau to his mother, December 3, 1867, in Houzeau Papers. For a discussion of the Afro-American delegates and their role in the convention, see Vincent, *Black Legislators*, 47–70.

161. The Louisiana Constitutional Convention was not the first "official assembly" of Negroes and whites in the United States. A racially mixed constitutional convention first met in Alabama, for instance, on November 5, 1867. See Peter Kolchin, *First Freedom: The Responses of Alabama's Blacks to Emancipation and Reconstruction* (Westport, Conn., 1972), 167.

white man, after all, should be the master. We shall survive this
mixed convention; it is a poor joke, but certainly one that will
never happen twice."

Now, this convention went on to write a state constitution
magnificent for its liberal principles. It ordained government of
the people, by the people—by all the people—without distinction of race, color, or religion, freedom of conscience and of religion, freedom of thought and opinion, freedom of speech and of
the press, the right of free assembly, the complete and entire freedom to work and to negotiate salaries, the right to form associations, the right to public and speedy trial, the right to bail except
in the case of a capital crime, equality before the law, the avail-
ability of public offices to all citizens, the right to common schools
for the children of both races. Finally, to correct strange local
abuses that the European reader would have difficulty understanding, it ordered that all be admitted, without distinction of
color, to public transportation and public places, and established
the principle that the merchant does not have the right to refuse to
sell his goods to any person.[162]

The division of executive, legislative, and judicial powers was
set forth in general terms according to the most liberal principles.
This constitution, taken as a whole, can serve as a model. Needless to say, it was accepted by Congress. It was under the aegis of
this agreement that Louisiana reentered the Union.[163] Elections
soon followed for the Federal legislative chambers. The common
sense of the "new voters" once again guided them. A black, Mr.
Menard, a man of brilliant intelligence, was elected by one of New
Orleans' districts, and he was first to plant the flag of the pro-

162. Ratified on April 16–17, 1868, the Louisiana Constitution of 1868 was
one of the most liberal drawn up under the Reconstruction Acts. Taylor, *Louisiana
Reconstructed*, 147–60.

163. Congress readmitted Louisiana to the Union on June 25, 1868.

scribed race in the Congress of the United States.[164] A naturalized Frenchman, Mr. Michel Vidal, who had worked at the *Tribune*, was sent to Washington by the vote of the men of color of Lafourche Parish. He owed his election to the position he had held on the newspaper.[165]

The coming to power of this new class—numerous, powerful, hardworking, yet only a few years before so severely and deeply downtrodden—was a magnificent sight. Our hearts rejoiced at the tardy and yet so nobly conceived and thoroughly executed reparation of long-standing injustice and nameless oppression. If

164. A descendant of the first lieutenant governor of Illinois, John Willis Menard was born in Kaskaskia, Illinois, on April 3, 1838. Educated at Iberia College in Ohio, Menard was a bold advocate of black emigration to Africa. In 1863 he pointedly reminded Frederick Douglass that "this is a *white* nation; white men are the engineers over its varied machinery and destiny; every dollar spent, every drop of blood shed and every life lost, was a *willing* sacrifice for the furtherance and perpetuity of a white nationality. . . . Sir, the inherent principle of the *white majority* of this nation is to refuse FOREVER republican equality to the black minority." Menard settled in New Orleans in 1865, and on November 3, 1868, apparently won election to the U.S. House of Representatives from the Second Congressional District of Louisiana. His election contested, Menard was never seated, but he was allowed to address Congress, the first Afro-American ever to do so. In 1871 Menard moved to Florida where he edited the Key West *Florida News* and Jacksonville *Southern Leader*. He died in Washington, D.C., on October 8, 1893. See Menard's volume of poetry, *Lays in Summer Lands* (Washington, D.C., 1879); Edith Menard, "John Willis Menard: First Negro Elected to the U.S. Congress, First Negro to Speak in the U.S. Congress," *Negro History Bulletin*, XXVIII (1964), 53–54; Bess Beatty, "John Willis Menard: A Progressive Black in Post–Civil War Florida," *Florida Historical Quarterly*, LIX (1980), 123–43. The 1863 quotation is from Joan R. Sherman, *Invisible Poets: Afro-Americans of the Nineteenth Century* (Urbana, 1974), 99.

165. *Now Consul of the United States at Tripoli.*—HOUZEAU. Born in France in 1824, Michel Vidal represented the Fourth Congressional District of Louisiana from July, 1868–March, 1869. He had previously been a member of the 1867–1868 state constitutional convention and a contributing editor to the St. Landry *Progress*. Although the *Tribune* praised Vidal as a man of "fairness and urbanity" in April, 1867, it later denounced him as the scoundrel responsible for Henry Clay Warmoth winning the Republican nomination for governor in 1868. Vidal served as American consul at Tripoli from 1870 until his death in 1876. *Tribune*, April 28, 1867; *Biographical Directory*, 1858; Geraldine M. McTigue, "Forms of Racial Interaction in Louisiana, 1860–1880" (Ph.D. dissertation, Yale University, 1975), 177–78, 257–58, 275.

we had cast stones at the United States because it had tolerated slavery, how we could praise it for the way in which it set things right! On November 14, 1864, when I began at the *Tribune*, would I ever have believed in so quick a triumph, even if it had been revealed to me in a prophetic vision? On March 18, 1868, when the Louisiana [Constitutional] Convention adjourned,[166] all that we could have conceived and asked for in the legal sphere had been accomplished.

It shall always be a great satisfaction to me to have played a part in the rehabilitation of five million men. From the point of view of philanthropy as well as that of social progress, this was without doubt the greatest event of our times. I witnessed a population as large as that of Belgium, and twice as large as that of Switzerland, given its freedom. I saw this crushed population lifted up bit by bit. Mothers, sisters, brothers, separated from their children, from their own brothers and sisters, came to the *Tribune* to ask for information concerning those whom the avarice of masters had removed from their affections. We reunited families: a mother discovered her son in a distant state, a sister found her brother whom she believed she would never see again. Sometimes names had been changed; in cases where the child had been taken away in his youth, it was almost impossible to trace his identity. What scenes of thanksgiving and inexpressible joy I witnessed then, and how often was I able to bless in my heart the principle of liberty![167]

166. The Louisiana Constitutional Convention adjourned on March 9, 1868.
167. Houzeau wrote to his parents on May 24, 1865, that "the reconstitution of families has not yet been completely accomplished. . . . There are children who were sold young and who have no recollection of their parents nor any identifying mark that would help them find them. They were taken far away and their names changed. There are still many mothers who have not been able to locate their sons or daughters. The notices that one sees everywhere or that one hears read in the churches contain material for a hundred novels that would be interesting, touching, and often mixed with details of an incredible brutality. When all this was going on not much was known about it, and even less said. Now that it is ancient

One day a freedman, sold during the days of slavery by the Trudeau family, whose tale of woe I told in the *Revue britannique* of 1863,[168] came to the *Tribune* in search of his parents. If emancipation had not repaired the harm done by this infamy, at least it ended the suffering of this infamy's victims. As a member of the board of directors of the Freedmen's Aid Association,[169] I participated in the early efforts to assure these ex-slaves their independence as men. We tried to teach people who were on their own for the first time how to take their first steps as free men. We found land, tools, grain, and credit for them; we taught them that they were men and that they could walk alone. Then once the government had provided land for this purpose, I had the satisfaction of serving as vice-president of the Louisiana Homestead Association, which sought to help those who wanted to farm to establish themselves.[170] Several villages were formed that will be the foun-

---

history one will no longer think to write about it, or one will soon forget about it. But a portrait of slavery in the United States would contain many hideous features. . . . But I see, dear parents, that I am carrying on about a very lugubrious subject. But what can I do; I see and hear nothing but that." A year and a half later, on November 18, 1866, Houzeau wrote to his mother on the same topic: "I certainly take to heart the general interest of an oppressed and disinherited class. I take interest in the great individual misfortunes—the mothers who look for their children who have been sold who knows where or when under the slavery régime; the sons who have become workers and are earning money who look for their old parents to shelter them from need." Both in Houzeau Papers. Articles chronicling the persistent but often futile efforts of freedmen to reunite their families appeared regularly in the *Tribune*. See, for example, the issues of June 16, 1865 (French ed.), March 7, 1866.

168. Houzeau, "Étude sur la guerre d'Amérique: Question de l'esclavage," *Revue britannique* (édition franco-belge), II (1863), 307–308.

169. See above, 110n.

170. The Louisiana Homestead Association was formed to assist loyal citizens in obtaining land under the Southern Homestead Act of June 21, 1866. "What we need, to democratize (in the true sense of the word) the Southern States," Houzeau wrote in 1867, "is to give to the middle class the facility of buying land, establishing small farms and cultivating land on a small scale. The time of large plantations has passed away. We want to found the independence of the newly enfranchised citizens on the possession and cultivation of land." The association failed, how-

dation of garden agriculture in the southern states. The black soldier, having returned to work and now owning his own home, farms for himself as a sharecropper the land that he had hitherto watered with the sweat of his brow for his master's profit. Like the soldier of the Roman legions, he has set his arms down by his hearth, ready to take them up again in defense of his freedom. He is a citizen, he has a say in the selection of magistrates and in the conduct of public affairs. Because the homeland has the right to call upon him to shed his blood in the defense of its institutions and its territory, is it not right that this man have a vote in the decisions of his nation? In any democratic government the right to vote is as inseparable from the status of being a soldier as from that of being a taxpayer.

Instead of having five million slaves, the United States today has five million devoted and hardworking citizens. Instead of ignorant masses, a generation is growing up that will have gone to school and benefited from the fruit of learning. Before another thirty years elapse, the traces of this regrettable past will have completely disappeared. How fulfilling it was to have participated in such a reform. How meaningful it was to have been involved, even if only as an instrument, in this great humanitarian movement.

The *Tribune* had served as the "official organ" of the [constitutional] convention of 1867. It had been chosen by the majority in a truly dramatic meeting,[171] despite the intrigues of the *Republican*. This newspaper, still incapable of any generous sentiment, failed to understand that, in order to guarantee equality among

ever, in its efforts to establish a large class of independent Negro farmers. A recent study estimates that from January, 1867, through December, 1870, only about fifty Afro-American families in the entire state of Louisiana successfully fulfilled the requirements for land under the Southern Homestead Act. *Tribune*, December 20, 1867; Claude F. Oubre, *Forty Acres and a Mule: The Freedmen's Bureau and Black Land Ownership* (Baton Rouge, 1978), 135.

171. The *Tribune* describes this important meeting on November 27, 1868.

races, it was necessary at the beginning to choose blacks because they were blacks.[172]

After many struggles the *Tribune* thus scaled the summit of success. Having sprung up from weak and humble origins—almost as lowly as the Negro on the plantation—long considered by the general population as was the slave by his master, then later treated simply as a freed man, it had lifted itself up slowly alongside those pariahs it strove to rehabilitate by its labors. And while the worshippers of the past lost everything, it slowly came to the fore and triumphed along with the triumph of its people. Honor, wealth, and, I dare say, reputation came knocking on its door.

All this was the fruit of a three-year struggle. During this short interval a social transformation of immense importance had taken place. The changes that occurred so rapidly at that time have left in my mind the impression of a long succession of events. An entire book would be needed to tell the story of the group of men who worked at the *Tribune* at the time. By day or by night, in the office or in the street, in dangerous situations as well as safe ones, my colleagues were on the job. I cannot recall to mind the days of my association with them without feeling sincere admiration for so much effort, devotion, and energy. These men must be at peace with their consciences, for they acquitted their duties nobly, and in uplifting their race they contributed to the good of their country. My memories thus turn with gratitude toward the small group of men from whom I received, in the most difficult times, true encouragement, and toward the men of both races who during different phases of this campaign shared with

172. The *Tribune* vigorously supported the decision of the Republican party in June, 1867, to guarantee that one half of all appointments and nominations go to Negroes. If candidates were chosen independent of race and solely on merit, the *Tribune* argued, Negro candidates would because of prejudice always be deemed unqualified. *Tribune*, June 18, July 6, 1867.

me their wise counsel and advice. Let my public thanks here join those that I previously gave in private.

It only remains for me to recount the final scene of my participation in this militant work. Once the constitution was written, it was necessary to elect a state government. In the United States it is customary that the candidate for each party be selected by an assembly of delegates, which we call here a "nominating convention." The Republican party held its convention.[173] Unfortunately, the colored delegates lacked familiarity with the men running for office. Similarly, they lacked political experience. This was the first time that they had exercised such difficult and important roles. They did not take the proper care to research the background of the candidates or to evaluate fully the worth of their characters.

There was thus much to criticize, much to regret in the list prepared by this assembly. Some shady individuals appeared on it. Some were hypocrites who groveled for the votes of the supporters of equal rights without having the least intention of keeping their promises. Experience has since borne this out. The "new electors" were won over by the flattery of ambitious men without worth. Aristophanes' scene about the *demopithecus* who gained popular support either through fraud or flattery was replayed before them, and they let themselves be taken in by it.[174]

The owners and the friends of the *Tribune* were so consternated by the judgment of their people that this irritation carried the day. Dr. Roudanez immediately spoke to me about submitting a different electoral list. But after accepting the authority of the

173. The Republican State Nominating Convention and the election of 1868 are discussed above, 47–56.

174. The reference is to Aristophanes, *The Frogs*, where *demopithecon* is found in the genitive plural and defined by Stanford in his commentary as "people who use the shameless antics and flatteries of monkeys to get popular power." Aristophanes, *The Frogs*, ed. W. B. Stanford (London, 1958), 167.

"nominating convention," how could we logically reject its verdict? Furthermore, what right had we to present candidates to oppose those of our own party? The delegates' faith had been misplaced, but they still believed in their illusions. If we were to submit other candidates solely on our own authority, we would only be setting our own personal wishes against those of the people's delegates. At the same time we would create a split in the Louisiana Republican party, a split that could lead to its defeat at the polls. Thus, we would be held responsible for this defeat in the eyes of the liberal party of the whole country. On the other hand, the prestige that comes from being nominated through regular channels would remain with the candidates of the nominating convention, and if we were to propose another list, this list would be defeated: the people would not follow us. Thus it would be the *Tribune* that would lose. Its moral authority, its reputation for common sense, all the influence it had acquired would fall at a single blow. These nominations were regrettable without any doubt, but did they necessitate the destruction of one's own party? Even more, was it necessary to destroy one's own sword? For to place ourselves on the outside of those whom we had always helped and led would be to place ourselves in a situation where we would cease to be useful to them.

Would it not be preferable to limit ourselves to making a protest, while remaining loyal to the rest of the party? We had merely to state: "These men intend to trick you; let our protest against such nominations be heard. Nevertheless, because the rest of the party wants them, let these men be tried out; experience alone will enlighten you."

The politics of independent action seemed to me so ill advised that I decided, decided definitively, not to get involved from the first words of our conversation. Finding me unshakable, the owners authorized me to follow whatever course I found preferable. But at the same time, they did not agree with me. For me, it was a delicate matter, for I did not wish to involve the newspaper in any way in a cause not approved of by its owners. My colored friends and I could only walk together if we chose the same road. It was not my place to force on them, despite themselves, a plan of action for the defense of their own cause. I was, of course, honored by their confidence, but various considerations led me to decline their offer. I declared, therefore, that I would stay out of the struggle.

During these three years I had written twelve large volumes, half in English, half in French, for the *Tribune*, not to mention all the business correspondence. The work had been endless. No week went by when I did not furnish at least sixteen columns; often my share rose to eighteen or twenty, and on one occasion I provided as many as twenty-three columns. I had not had one day's vacation, with the exception only of Sundays, when all American newspapers take a day off. Anyone who has worked steadily for a daily newspaper will know how tired I felt. As soon as I decided not to get involved, I also decided to leave the country.

I had put a vast amount of toil into establishing the newspaper, and now that it was about to undo itself, I did not feel that I wanted to lift it up again after its fall and to begin all over the task of reestablishing it—a labor that would be more difficult and less appreciated than the first.[175] It would, in fact, be recently defeated and very unpopular. I resigned the editorship on January 18, 1868. On February 19 the newspaper, judged thereafter to be dissident, was removed from the list of official newspapers of the United States. This was an immense loss both in terms of prestige and financial support. The *Tribune* was also repudiated by all Re-

175. Houzeau wrote to his parents on May 9, 1868: "There was no question of reviving the *Tribune* or the press. For myself, I would not help not only because I am leaving but because they cast to the wind the good reputation that I had made for them and the advantages that I had acquired for them." In Houzeau Papers.

publican associations, and it was thus forced to abandon the title of "official organ" of the party. This title was given instead to its white rival, the *Republican*. Furthermore, the election confirmed my fears. The battle became so unequal that the *Tribune*'s candidates withdrew just as the balloting began. Discredited in the eyes of its former supporters, the newspaper itself ceased to appear on April 25.

We can hereby see how quickly events follow one another in the United States. Although the "colored newspaper" has since lifted up its banner again, the lost ground has not yet been regained. The new *Tribune*, now only a weekly newspaper, even though it has lost its position as an official newspaper of the United States, has once again taken up its work with courage worthy of a better end. The old *Tribune* had fallen the day after the conquest of political rights, when the work to which it had dedicated itself seemed accomplished. Not all has yet been said, however. Societies are like travelers: the more they travel forward, the more new horizons open before their eyes. The old *Tribune* lived long enough to see equality under the law triumph. The new *Tribune* will have to fight to obtain equality among the customs and habits of daily life in society.

Indeed, it is now necessary to infuse public mores with the same spirit that enacted the laws. For without reform of the mores, implementation of the laws is nearly impossible, or illusory. "We make laws," says Lady Montagu, "but we follow customs."[176]

Quid leges sine moribus vanæ proficiunt?[177]

176. The quotation is from Lady Mary Wortley Montagu (1689–1762), the British letter-writer, poet, and essayist. It was apparently one of Houzeau's favorites, for he used it in the *Tribune* on May 8, 1866, and again on April 26, 1867.

177. "Of what avail are empty laws, if we lack principle." Horace, *The Odes and Epodes*, trans. C. E. Bennett (London, 1960), 255.

So long as the most influential part of the population is hostile to the great principle of equal rights and justice for all, such equality, such justice, will only exist precariously as an exception.

The new *Tribune* marches to this last battle with the same energy, the same boldness, that the founders of the newspaper revealed during the worst days of old. The necessity of the situation will surely produce a man who will carry out this new campaign and who will banish the spirit of caste from society.

Appendix

DEAR AUGUSTE,[1]

European newspapers have probably described—if only in a few vague words—the frightful events that occurred here last Monday, July 30, in which several hundred people died. The next day I wrote our parents to reassure them of my safety. This letter will serve as a duplicate in case the first is lost in the mail.

You know that each state in the Union possesses legislative authority in its own sphere: both federal and state laws and courts operate concurrently, as you [in Belgium] have both civil and commercial laws and courts. In 1864, Louisiana held a convention to rewrite its constitution, and this convention abolished slavery in the state legal system. At the time of its last meeting in July, 1864, the convention did not dissolve itself but rather empowered its president to reconvene it to enact further reform measures. Recently, many members called for a new meeting, but the convention's president refused to reconvene it and left the state.

The members, therefore, met on their own authority and without a quorum; they elected a president *pro tempore* who reconvened the assembly for July 30. This procedure was highly irregular; but if a quorum was present on July 30, the assembly clearly could resume its activities, having reconvened itself: the assembly had at least as much authority as its own presiding officer. Fur-

---

1. Jean-Charles Houzeau to Auguste Houzeau, August 5, 1866, in Jean-Charles Houzeau Papers, Centre National d'Histoire des Sciences, Bibliothèque Royale Albert 1ᵉʳ, Brussels, Belgium.

thermore, the governor authorized this meeting when he ordered special elections to be held on September 3, to fill the vacant seats.

On July 30, the convention was scheduled to meet and then to adjourn until after these elections. One single law—very important for these special elections—was scheduled to be enacted; this was the proclamation of universal suffrage, which would enfranchise the blacks. The justifications and the terms of the decree had been printed on my printing presses; only enough copies were printed for the Republican members. The proposal had been written and would be presented by one of my good friends, a doctor of Scottish origin who is now in bed with a dagger wound in the side and a bullet in the head.

The proslavery forces with the help of the mayor, elected by white suffrage alone, and his police drawn from the scum of every nation could not prevent this event, which was very popular among the blacks who constituted half of the state's population. They therefore laid plans for a sort of Sicilian Vespers. It was easy to reach this decision since hatred of blacks is in the heart of every defender of slavery. They kept their secret well; the most we expected was that they would challenge the validity of the law in the courts.

The convention was scheduled to meet at noon. Just imagine an immense second-floor hall, approximately 25 by 40 meters in size; the public in the section behind the bar; the members had to pass through it to reach their places—a group of plain chairs set off from the others by their semicircular arrangement; at the back of the hall a platform on which rested three tables, arranged in the shape of a horseshoe: the president's in the center; to his right the secretary and his assistants; and at the table to his left, a long and narrow one, were both local and visiting journalists. I was seated at this last table.

The meeting convened at the stroke of noon in the presence of a few hundred black spectators—two or three hundred more blacks were waiting in the street below, a normal occurrence here when there is a political meeting. There was no quorum when the roll was called; the meeting was adjourned briefly to wait for the arrival of latecomers. I had left my seat and had begun to chat with a succession of different people when the sound of sporadic gunfire, becoming more regular, was heard from the street. It was an organized attack, and since few of us were armed, it was hard to repulse it. The crowd in the street held it off with stones for an entire half hour. We watched the fighting from the windows. The crowd was caught in a crossfire, and we were prisoners since the attack had been launched simultaneously from both ends of the street.

After some time the crowd retreated into our building, and we hoped that this would end the engagement. But since the attackers had felt their ranks too few to attack the hall, the mayor had a prearranged signal rung from the bell in city hall—a tocsin like the one that announced the St. Bartholomew's Day Massacre; and five hundred policemen armed with revolvers lent their assistance to the assault. They were resisted as much as possible. The gunfire increased to an average rate of four shots per second. The crowd barricaded itself in the building, and many were killed when the assassins broke the doors down and forced entry into the hall. A few jumped out of windows at the risk of their lives only to be massacred in the courtyard below. I knew about a service staircase behind the president's chair; several other people and I used it to reach a small yard below, from which I searched open passageways for a way out.

Near the main entrance I found blacks armed with stones, preparing to fight the attackers; there were many dead and wounded among them. Reversing direction I heard a friend calling to me; he was jumping over a waist-high wall. And I then climbed over this barrier as best I could. We found ourselves in a furniture-maker's shop, which opened on the street behind the hall. The cannonade of revolver fire (if you will permit me the usage) was very heavy on this street, which contained a crowd being fired upon from both sides.

At first I removed my suit coat and set myself to work next to a laborer. Soon, however, many other people found this shop in the same way that I had, and I foresaw that the fighting, or rather the massacre, would follow and eventually come into the shop. I peeked through the door standing ajar—the shop was closed; and I saw a shoe store directly across the street whose owner was sneaking a peek as I was. He was someone I knew. He recognized me, signaled me to come over, and in a flash I made it across the street to his shop. I remained there until the end of the massacre. I was only able to continue to watch what was happening through the key hole and the bolts.

The people in the streets were being beaten and shot at point-blank range; they were chased into houses to the accompaniment of wild shouts. The heads of the wounded lying on the ground were crushed. The houses next to the hall where the convention was held were attacked and captured; all their inhabitants without distinction were killed. Policemen in a frenzy stopped [horse-drawn] buses and killed any blacks found on them, including children. When I had left the meeting hall, [those trapped] had begun to rip out the floor to board up the windows to protect themselves from the bullets that had already broken all the window glass and hit many people. Once the door to the hall was beaten in, the ensuing carnage was beyond all description. The mayor, a worthless man who cannot spell, a vile instrument of the proslavery terrorists of 1861, who had been a dockworker, directed the massacre. United States troops are quartered outside the city; they arrived on the scene at 3:30, when no one was left to be killed.

What prolonged the struggle is that revolvers at twenty paces do not make serious wounds; at ten paces there are still no fatal wounds. One unexpected fact struck me: rarely does a wounded person cry out, and even after very serious wounds a man can get up and walk except in the most serious cases. What was the most hideous were the yells and calls of these savages whenever a defenseless man fell!

Simultaneously a campaign of assassination, isolated assassinations, directed against Union supporters, was carried out throughout the city. I heard the shout "To the *Tribune!*," and I feared to find the presses destroyed. They were protected by a company of black soldiers. Some of the typesetters had fled and were threatened at home. All my employees, save one, had fled. I sat at my desk, and I alone wrote the English description of the events, then the French description together with thoughts inspired by these events. Then came the task of informing all our friends in the North and in the West by telegraph, of listening to the information volunteered by everyone, of sending the members of Congress a more complete description of what happened, of being in constant communication with the generals. Terror still reigns over the outlying sections of the city. My coworkers have not returned yet.

I have insisted on not only continuing to publish but on revealing everything. In the past six days I have written twenty-eight columns of original material in both English and French; I have written and dispatched an immense correspondence; and I have questioned two hundred witnesses in a preliminary manner in order to send the most useful to the War Office. On some days I worked twenty hours. Yesterday, Saturday, at seven in the evening, was the first time since Monday that I was able to sit at table for a meal. I never saw such cold-blooded horrors, and you can well imagine that the director of the colored press, the erstwhile

160

Appendix

author of *La terreur blanche*,[2] would have had twenty assassins
ready to strike him on the spot should he have shown his face.

The board of directors of the printing plant voted me its
thanks and immediately increased my salary, so that I now earn
very close to fourteen thousand francs.

The effect in the North is immense; it will probably be almost
as great as that of Lincoln's assassination. The guilt of the mayor
and his police will be proven beyond all doubt; moreover, it is also
probable that the lieutenant governor, the attorney general, and a
state judge will be convicted of having been accomplices—to be
more accurate, instigators and organizers. These are proslavery
advocates of the worst kind. In Europe it must be difficult to understand why such highly placed, rich men, belonging to the upper
strata of society, support something so despicable. It is the effect
of a long possession of man by man. The moral sense is destroyed, in every respect. These men do not see themselves committing a crime. For them this is a little preventive antidote
against the reformers and the anarchists.

You can well understand that after the abolition of slavery, the
idea of excluding blacks, now free, from the rights accorded by law
to other citizens is impossible. These come to men as a necessary
by-product of American institutions. A citizen must have all the
rights of the citizen or he is only a mock citizen. I can understand
that voters of every color should be required to meet specific conditions, for example, that they be able to read; but to maintain today
that a voter must come from the white race without admixture is
completely absurd. There are blacks and mulattoes who are very
well qualified to hold public office. Is it not now necessary to open

2. J.-C. Houzeau, *La terreur blanche au Texas et mon évasion* (Brussels, 1862).
This abolitionist tract, which originally appeared in slightly different form in the
Revue trimestrielle, describes Houzeau's battle with proslavery vigilantes in Texas in
1861–62.

schools and colleges to all? The convention had planned to institute these reforms; they nevertheless will come about because they
are a necessity of social evolution. A majority of the Convention of
1864 supported us; it had been elected under very strong military
pressure, and at a time when many secessionists abstained from the
polls. Elections held today under the old (white) suffrage law return proslavery fanatics throughout Louisiana.

I received your letter Tuesday. I looked at your photographs
this morning. I shall write concerning this in a few days. Give my
best wishes to everyone.

JEAN

Index

152; and constitutional convention of 1867–68, p. 147

Union, L' (New Orleans), 19–23, 19–20n, 21n, 34–35, 35n, 38n, 71–72, 71nn, 76n, 140n
Uzo, Carles [pseudonym of Houzeau], 11

Vidal, Michael, 144, 144n

Wallace, Alfred R., 13
Warmoth, Henry Clay, 47, 48, 48n, 49, 55, 55n, 56, 116, 116n, 144n
Wells, J. Madison, 126, 126n